Photo by Chantek McNeilage.

RESCUE AND RECOVERY

Iskra's ordeal in the Hebrides

Frank Mulville

SEAFARER BOOKS

SHERIDAN HOUSE

First published in 1997
by Seafarer Books
an imprint of Merlin Press
2 Rendlesham Mews, Rendlesham, Woodbridge, Suffolk IP12 2SZ

in the USA by Sheridan House
145 Palisade Street, Dobbs Ferry, N.Y. 10522

ISBN 085036 462 0

Maps drawn by Tony Garrett

Cover design: Louis Mackay

Cover painting: Dick Everitt

Layout and typesetting by Priory Publications, Haywards Heath.

Printed in England by FotoDirect Ltd, Brighton

Contents

To Adrian

and to our friends in Gigha

who helped us.

"There's a divinity that shapes our ends,
Rough-hew them how we will."

Shakespeare

1

Fair Winds

It was not an easy beginning to a voyage. We had flogged our way down channel against a relentless wind, varying in direction from north-west to south-west and in strength from force 4 to force 6. We were all tired of it. Wendy was tired of it, I was tired of it, *Iskra* was tired of it. We had gained what respite we could, in Ramsgate at the beginning and then in Alderney and Guernsey just over half way to Ushant, the western corner of France. Surely now, as we turned south towards Spain, the wind would come fair for us – we felt we deserved a fair wind. We had been tacking back and forth across the channel for six days to gain a paltry 260 miles. With a good fair wind we would have romped it in two.

Sailing down channel against the prevailing westerlies is one price we pay for the privilege of living on the east coast of England – the channel is our Rubicon. Often the wind blows remorselessly out of the south-west for days, even weeks on end. Then it is difficult, bordering on impossible, to sail *Iskra* through the Straits of Dover and on the long haul between Dover and the west of France. If you have a fair tide it is running against the wind and sets up a chop which effectively slows the boat to a crawl. When the tide runs the other way the sea smooths itself but the tide sets you back. There is nowhere to anchor for miles, few places to go in, nowhere to rest. A big, powerful boat with a strong crew can do it. *Iskra* can do it but only with discomfort. In the days of sail, ships bound to the west would anchor in the Downs off Deal to wait for a fair wind; sometimes they could be numbered in hundreds.

We came up with Ushant in the night. The wind fell light and then died to a whisper, soon leaving us becalmed in the

Atlantic swell, the great light sweeping the horizon, beckoning us to the south. It had in it both threat and promise – fair winds, the warming sun, the thrill of foreign landfalls or the scalding gales and tumbling seas of the Bay of Biscay, the coast of France a rock-bound threat to leeward. As *Iskra* lay rolling aimlessly in the ocean swell it seemed as if the light was holding us in its palm, scrutinising us with its baleful wink, weighing up whether to hurl us into the maelstrom or exalt us to the nirvana of a fair wind. I tapped the barometer, it gave a slight start, a shudder, neither up nor down, undecided and unable to make up its mind. It was a low glass – it hadn't moved for four days. The sky was overcast as it had been for a week, there was a feeling of nervous apprehension. Wendy was in her bunk but not asleep. I made her a cup of tea, sat for a minute holding her warm hand. Thus far it had not been a pleasant voyage for her. She had been seasick for a spell but it had passed. 'One day feeling sick, one day being sick and one day recovering' was the pattern. The sun had been a brief visitor, the motion, bucking into a head sea, uncomfortable, tiring. There had been shipping to be kept clear of, always a trial to her. She imagines every ship is determined to run us down, bent on our destruction. Now there was this feeling of tension in the air.

"Is it going to blow?," she asked.

"I don't see why it should. The forecast said nothing bad, nothing good either for that matter. There's a low about and a high. It depends on which one takes over I suppose."

Iskra was beginning to slip back as the flood tide up channel caught her in its grip, the light slowly changing its bearing. It was about 6 miles off to port. I started the engine and ran it slow, more to stop her from going backwards than to make headway, dropped the heads'ls and pinned in the main sheet to stop the boom from crashing back and forth as she rolled. It was just after three in the morning, Wendy came on watch. With the engine running in a calm, there is no wind to work the vane and *Iskra* must be steered. I gave her the course, made sure she was warm.

"It's not really a very nice voyage so far," she said ruefully, "I hope it's going to get better – hope it's not going to end in some great disaster."

"I'm sure it's not – why should it? You're letting your imagination go haywire."

"I don't know – it all looks a bit threatening."

"Nonsense – if it does start blowing from the south-west we'll tuck ourselves in somewhere in Brittany and wait for it to get better."

It was an unnerving night, it was hard to pin it down but I couldn't deny it to myself. I went to my bunk. The even beat of the old engine did its best to send me to sleep but I was restless. If it did blow hard from the west it wouldn't be easy to find a safe anchorage. The Brittany coast is rock bound and beset by strong tides. To get there we would have to thread our way through a maze of rocks and small islands inside Ushant Island. Equally, I had no wish to set off across Biscay in contrary or threatening weather. Now it was my imagination – dragging up forebodings out of nothing. I went to sleep.

We were bound for Santander in Spain. The idea had come to me on a cold January Saturday morning in 1992. There was snow on *Iskra*'s green winter cover, a biting east wind. For some reason the idea of Spain swam into my mind. I was working inside, changing the injectors in the engine ready for the new season. Working on the engine, or any work inside the boat in winter time, allows the mind to range free, embracing all manner of subjects and journeying through time and space, in and out of every kind of fantasy. Sometimes the mind fixes itself on a single idea, or project, or a scheme takes root and the seeds of a voyage are sown. Wendy had never been to Altamira to see the cave paintings; I had been there once, years ago. Some whiff of nostalgic Spanish air must have been left behind in the recesses of *Iskra*'s cabin to awake an old memory. I finished the injectors, made my way home.

"I've never seen them," Wendy said. "Yes, I would like to."

3

I told her about the great bison painted on the roof of the cave, the deer, the running bulls, the wonderful fresh feeling of vigour and movement which the figures convey. We had no particular plan in our minds for the summer, no enterprises knocking at our door. "All right, we'll get *Iskra* fitted out and go to Spain – then we'll take her to Brest '92."

I found, on enquiry, that it is no longer easy to visit the paintings. When I first went to Altamira the caves were almost deserted. We found a sleepy guide who showed us round for a few pesetas. Now, we were lucky to find a place in the waiting list six months in advance. Now, a tourist industry has sprung up round the caves. The number of visitors has been restricted because the atmosphere in the caves was being changed by the press of people, to the detriment of the paintings. There is an exhibition centre with graphic explanations; groups of five tourists are taken round, quite quickly, and there is a gap between each group. The atmosphere is carefully monitored and controlled.

Wendy woke me at dawn. "There's wind," she said, "it came up ten minutes ago – from the west." It was still heavily overcast, the breeze was from dead ahead, the light on Ushant was still on our port bow, a little nearer perhaps. I set the heads'ls again and we turned off the engine. On the starboard tack *Iskra* headed for the island, we could see its iron shore through the early light. There was no hope of weathering it. On the port tack we pointed in the general direction of Land's End. "We'll have to flog on for an hour or so," I said.

The wind increased, the tide turned in our favour. It began to get rough, *Iskra* plunging into the steep seas, throwing spray over the deck. The same old punch into the wind, the same old waves in endless procession, the same stinging spray, the same discomfort – sailing is sometimes a discouraging business. "It's got to get better – once we can weather the island we'll be able to ease the sheet." My optimism sounded hollow, even to me.

Wendy saw it first. I was standing at the galley, making a hot drink, she was sitting in the hatch, collar buttoned up, sou'wester pulled down. "Come and look at this." To the north the cloud was lifting, a strip of blue had fattened itself until it had swelled over half the heavens. I looked at the barometer. Had it moved, ever so slightly up? I tapped it and it jumped up. The wind was working quickly round to the north – we eased the sheet, turned towards the south, bringing the island broad on the bow. *Iskra* began to move fast, falling into the easy rhythm of a fair wind. "Fair wind for Spain," I shouted, "Come on – we're off."

Soon the wind came strong from the NNE, no mistaking it now. As soon as we were clear of the racing tides round Ushant we set twin stays'ls and *Iskra* was really on her way. Life transformed itself. The mains'l was taken down, the heavy boom stowed on the gallows, the course set on the vane steering. She runs true with the twins, like a square-rigged ship, helm amidships, no strain, no fear of a gybe. The two white sails seem to lift her, skim her over the waves. When a good fair wind comes after days of frustration the whole aspect of life changes. There is a new outlook of vigour and hope and a surging joy that seems to envelop us. Wendy smiles with the happy prospect of a landfall. I make wild, optimistic calculations of our estimated time of arrival, the log spins busily, the sea zips past, *Iskra* cleaves the ocean like a queen.

These are rare moments of perfection, when life conspires to our advantage. The sun shines, great white clouds stack the sky, the wind is fair, our boat gives of her best, dolphins play round the bow, storm petrels weave patterns in the sky across our stern, we have all we need, all we want. In each other we hold a mirror to ourselves. The quest for perfection is the purpose of all endeavour. We find it, or fail to find it, in our own peculiar ways. Our view of what it comprises is as varied as are the means by which we seek it.

Wendy believes that the story of the Garden of Eden is prophetic rather than historic, that the Garden is all around us now. When she observes the opening of a spring bud, or traces the intricate markings of a leaf or watches a worm or a spider about his business, she marvels at the subtle wisdom of nature. When we watch the dolphins round *Iskra*'s bow, or a flight of fulmars racing across the wave tops, or gaze into the sun-drenched calm of the tropic ocean to observe the pulsating life before our eyes we are rendered speechless by the cleverness of it. The world is full of beauty and beauty is the fountainhead of perfection. Surely this must be paradise? It is human beings, lacking the wisdom of nature, who are unable to recognise paradise even though it is all around them. We are clever but we are short on wisdom. When Eve gave Adam the fruit from the tree of knowledge she gave him the means to destroy the tree of life, which he has been doing ever since.

We ran for two halcyon days under twins, across the continental shelf where the seas were rough enough to send Wendy to her bunk for a spell. We sailed into the centre of the Bay of Biscay, well inside the trade routes between Ushant and Cape Finisterre, clear of all shipping. We saw no sign of the dozens of French tunamen that used always to inhabit these waters – over-fishing has sent them further afield. It was like the tradewinds but it wasn't the tradewinds. We missed the flying fish, the tradewind clouds round the horizon in patterns of fantasy, the feeling of certainty and permanence of tradewind sailing. We knew that it could all end very quickly. The wind could go round to the north-west and ease or it could back round to the south-west and blow. For as long as we had it, we rejoiced. We settled into the routine very happily, eating, sleeping, keeping a lookout, watching the sky for signs of a change, taking sights morning and noon. There is something satisfying about routine and we never tire of watching the ocean. It is full of change and colour and interest.

A tiny bird came on board, this one straight from the Garden of Eden. He was all bright green and yellow, his head with a plume of white feathers, his unwinking eyes a deep, mysterious blue, his breast of the softest, purest white. The markings on his wings were a magic pattern of colour and symmetry, each wing repeating the design of its fellow with perfect accuracy. He was tired to exhaustion having flown from Ushant Island, or even from France. He was quite unafraid. He sat on Wendy's slipper and then, for a while, he moved to my knee. I could feel the imprint of his miniscule foot, a thing so perfectly shaped and formed that no improvement to it could be conceived, each delicate joint flexing and giving against the motion of the boat. He flew around the cabin, hopping from perch to perch investigating every detail of this strange bower he had strayed into, chirping in a friendly fashion with no trace of apprehension. He took a rest for a little while, perched on the cabin compass, its gimballed surface a steady platform for his perusal of our home. Then he accepted a drink of water from a saucer Wendy offered him, shook himself all over and took off. He perched on the life-line for a moment, then circled the boat once and set off bravely for France, some 10 miles distant, swerving and swooping with the wind currents, skimming the wave tops, guided by some inner magic of which we, with all our cleverness, have no understanding. He had brought us a brief spell of supreme happiness.

I have the feeling that I don't really own *Iskra* – she is not a possession, rather I am her carer. We look after each other and have done so for the last 25 years. She keeps me safe, I mend her gear, paint her, clean her, make her smart and see that her old bones are kept in good shape. She takes me where I want to go, I see to it that she is well provided for and safely berthed. She doesn't mind how far our journeys range or how long they take or whether they are to cold climes or hot – she is a hopeful traveller, not much concerned with arriving. Sometimes I am remiss in my side of the bargain. Through lassitude, or meanness, or forgetfulness I neglect to do for her what she ought to have done. When this happens she has a habit of pulling me up with a round turn, reminding me in some way that the bargain is not being kept. Usually the worse my remission, the sharper her protesting kick.

There is nothing remarkable in this relationship between

man and boat; it is as old as the sea. A boat, any boat, is inanimate whether it be made of wood or plastic or steel or concrete. It cannot feel, it cannot cry out either in pain or in ecstasy, it can't admonish or applaud; it simply takes what is given. This may be so, as far as it goes, but there is more to life than nuts and bolts. A boat is also a creation, a bringing together of knowledge, skills, traditions, devotion, inspiration. When all these things are joined so that a boat is conceived and comes into being, it attaches to itself another, less definable property. It takes on a spirit, a personality, a soul. Those who follow the sea are aware of this truth.

Iskra has grown in my affections over the past couple of decades and in Wendy's over one and a half decades, because of the experiences we have all been through together. The fact that she is what is now called a classic boat is irrelevant; when I bought her the breed had not been invented. I bought her because she suited my needs and because she was cheap. She has continued to meet my needs over the years and I have never had any desire to change her for another boat. Before I had owned her for very long I began to notice that she seems to have an instinct for her own and my preservation. She is a lucky ship – I know I must never bank on it. She has looked after me with unswerving fidelity, snatching herself and me from the brink of disaster time and time again. At first I put this down to pure chance, or to some quirk of fate, but as near squeak followed near squeak over the years, I began to believe that the fates had indeed smiled on her. After all, *Iskra* is framed in oak, planked with pitch pine, living substances with a mythology going back to the misty beginnings of history. Why should she not share in it?

She has shown me her lucky ways over and over again. I was by myself, sailing home from Denmark – I believe it was in 1978. After three days out across the North Sea we ran into a hard north-westerly gale and in the night, one of *Iskra*'s main shrouds broke. There was no damage to the mast. By doubling back the wire and fastening it with bulldog grips I was able to make a satisfactory repair. It was daylight by the time I had finished and she was back on course – I was cold and wet and tired. The gale had moderated but it was still blowing hard.

I changed my clothes and prepared for an hour's sleep but when I looked round the horizon I saw that *Iskra* had run into an oil field – the horizon was dotted with rigs for as far as the eye could reach. There were hundreds of them, sleep was not possible. At last the final platform came and went and I picked up the South Haisboro buoy and the low Norfolk coast. I was desperate for sleep. It was late afternoon, the tide was fair, the wind now a light, northerly breeze. In another hour we were within a mile of the shore, following the coast. I started the engine, there was just enough wind to keep her on course with the steering vane. The sea was calm, the flood tide was sweeping *Iskra* down into the narrow channels between Yarmouth's off-lying sands.

I put the kettle on, sat in the companion hatch on the bridge deck, my legs dangling inside. It was a lovely evening, quite cold, the sea a pale blue, a few white clouds motionless in the sky. Soon I heard the kettle's low persistent whistle. I went into the cabin, made tea in the little white teapot with roses on the lid.

It was snug and cosy and warm. The engine thumped rhythmically, a slight vibration, a relaxed purring, like a contented cat. I glanced at the chart – she had half an hour to run before the first buoy. I dropped into the soft luxury of my favourite seat, one arm over the chart table, one leg up on the settee, sipped my tea, glanced across at the cabin lamps gently shuffling in their gimbals with the engine's rattle. It had been a long sail from Tyboron, soon we would be tied up in harbour. Then I would sleep . . . sleep . . sleep . . .

For the next hour and ten minutes, *Iskra* and the engine piloted me through the shoals off Great Yarmouth. I don't know whether they took me inside the Caister bank, where the spring flood races south in a torrent of small tidal wavelets grumbling and grinding as it churns its way through the narrow cut, or outside and round the Scroby Elbow where drying banks are iron hard and the chart is riddled with wrecks.

Off Yarmouth, *Iskra* decided in her wisdom to carry on to Lowestoft, a better haven and a handful of miles nearer home. She followed the coast round to starboard, passed inside the West Corton and the Holm Sand, through the narrows off Lowestoft Ness and squared up for the green buoy at the harbour entrance. At that moment the engine stopped – I woke up with a jerk of alarm. The port fuel tank was empty. I had time to get the mains'l down, furl up the jib, change to the starboard tank and put the helm down to catch the last of the flood tide through the entrance, in the last of the daylight.

On another day she broke her mooring in Bradwell creek. It was blowing a south-westerly gale the top of a spring tide. It must have been a few minutes before high water, no one was about. Bradwell creek is a thick nest of moored yachts, all strewn across the fairway with a strong wind against tide, hardly a space to get through. Somehow *Iskra* was blown by the wind half way down the creek against the tide. She must have missed dozens of yachts by inches, weaved her way through them all without touching one. If she had a mind to, she could have wreaked expensive havoc with her bowsprit. Instead, she settled herself on a patch of soft mud off the hard.

She once dragged her anchor in Adalvic Bay in the north of Iceland when Wendy and I were fast asleep. We had come into the place on a misty night – except that there is no night on the Arctic Circle in mid summer. We anchored off the shore in poor visibility. Our chart was the best available but was small scale. When we woke up *Iskra* had moved herself across the bay, skirted a group of dangerous rocks and brought herself up in the only good anchorage, off a beach of volcanic sand.

Iskra is heavy for her 30ft overall length and her 10ft beam. Without her internal ballast, and without her mast and her gear, she tops 10¼ tons. All her planks run the full length of the ship, with no butt joints. They are of 1 inch thick, 5 inches

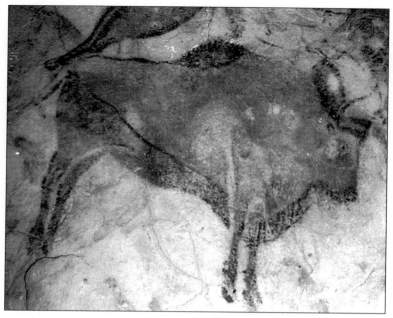

The great Bison of Altamira.

Running with twins – bliss.

Perched for a moment, then set off bravely.

Happy landfall.

wide pitch pine. It is one of the best, perhaps the best timber for planking up a boat, especially the longleaf variety of which *Iskra* is built. It was used extensively in English boat building between the wars. It is a lovely light, golden yellow colour with deep red markings due to the darker and denser summer growth of the tree. It is resinous, which protects it against salt water, as long lasting as oak itself and is flexible so that it can give to a sudden shock and then return to its original shape. At the same time it is durable and resistant to bruising. It is the strongest and heaviest of all the pines.

The tree grows in North America to a height of 80ft and is fully mature after 100 years of growth. *Iskra*'s trees would have been planted, or taken root, in the year 1800 or thereabouts. The wood has a distinct aroma when it is cut and the growth rings, alternate light and dark wood, are well defined. It is now almost impossible to obtain new pitch pine – sometimes it can be salvaged from old buildings.

Iskra's frames, her skeleton, the real core of her where her strength resides, are of English oak. Her timbers are of grown oak, following the natural curve and grain of the wood rather than being cut to shape. Where the branch of a tree grows out of the trunk, there the grown oak frames are fashioned for the greatest strength. Where frames are sawn, the grain is cross cut and its strength thereby reduced. *Iskra*'s ribs, which lie between the frames, are also of oak, 1¾ inches wide and 1¼ inches thick. These are cut from planks of new timber with the sap still in it. They are steamed and bent to shape.

The mythology attaching to oak dates back to ancient times. To the druids the oak, strong and long lived, was a sacred tree, as it was to the Scandinavians. The Argonaut's ship *Argo* was built of oak, one oak timber could speak and gave directions to the voyagers. Some of the largest trees standing in Britain are believed to date from Saxon times. At one time, England was covered in oak forest, an incredible and perhaps unmatched bequest by nature to the people of this land, as much responsible for shaping our history as our deposits of coal. The forests have been ruthlessly depleted over the centuries, sometimes quickly, sometimes slowly, but with a relentless momentum which has never wavered.

The building of a 74 gun ship in 1750 consumed 3,700 mature oak trees, the *Victory* required the felling of eighty acres of oak forest. Oak trees take at least one hundred years to mature; the average life of one of Nelson's ships of the line was no more than twenty years. Some were destroyed in battle, more were wrecked or foundered through neglect and poor maintenance. Our bequest is still being destroyed, often without just reason. *Iskra*'s dolphin figurehead is carved from a piece of oak, the trees her frames are fashioned from were saplings when Queen Victoria was a little girl.

Iskra's keel is of elm – strong, very tough, difficult to split and a good shock absorber. It has a twisted grain, is difficult to work due to knots, irregular growth and warping. It has always been used for the keels and keelsons of ships; it doesn't mind whether it is wet or dry. Her coach roof and her trim in the cockpit are of Burma teak, surely the most noble of woods. It is a rich brown in colour with a dense grain, oily and odorous, heavy and hard. The older it is the harder it becomes and the darker in colour. It tends to split. The coach roof has a split in it which has been there since I have owned her. An extra teak strut was fitted inside the cabin a few years ago to strengthen it. Her inside trim is not grand, mostly pine tongue and groove, nailed together. She was built to a price, the best materials and work going into her hull.

Wendy and I have been on board many fine plastic yachts and I have been on board a few concrete and steel yachts although I have never sailed one. Fibreglass is simple to maintain, steel is immensely strong, concrete is rot proof and easily repaired. My friend Dick Morris has created a magnificent yacht on a ferro-cement hull – strong, powerful, easily sailed, she is a monument to his energy and skill. One of Wendy's friends, Chris Thomas, had a steel yacht built for himself and sailed her in great comfort and safety across the world to Singapore. My brother Jack took his little fibreglass yacht to the West Indies and lived on board her for nearly seven years. I have no doubt that each of them holds his boat in as much affection as I hold *Iskra.*

My reason tells me there is nothing magic about wood, no hidden quality of excellence that sets it apart from all other materials. There are good and bad boats among them all. A good deal of snobbery attaches itself to the subject – it is considered a cut above, distinguished, to own a wooden boat. Certainly, plastic, steel, ferro-cement are all inert, lifeless substances which may not in themselves inspire admiration, respect, even love. Wood lives and breathes and is beautiful. A tree is one of the world's most astonishing wonders.

The Bay of Biscay slipped away under *Iskra*'s keel, watch followed watch, day followed day all too quickly. The ocean smiled, the wind held steady and true, the sun coursed through a clear, blue sky, dropped gently away when its time came, leaving a fleeting sheen of golden light over our world. This was our exclusive world, a sanctuary we shared only with the creatures of the ocean who are our companions and our friends. Soon the yellow moon heaved itself over the horizon, dimming the stars with its silver light, blazing a pathway across the sea to where *Iskra* sailed steadily on her way. The creak of rope through block, the easy lift and fall of a lazy sheet, the ocean's music, the masthead swinging across the heavens made whole this symphony of light and sound. We watched it all in silence – no words of ours could add to this wonder. I had never experienced such a crossing of the Bay of Biscay before.

As we neared the Spanish coast, the wind veered and eased, so that we rolled through the swell with just enough wind to keep *Iskra* moving. The twins were taken in and put away in the locker, under mains'l and tops'l and the big reaching heads'l she sailed peacefully towards Spain. Soon a darkening line across the southern horizon resolved itself into the Cordillera Cantabrica, the mountains of Northern Spain. We could hear the bleep from Cabo Mayor radio signal on our bow. We waited patiently through the afternoon until Cabo Mayor slipped past our starboard side. We came up with the

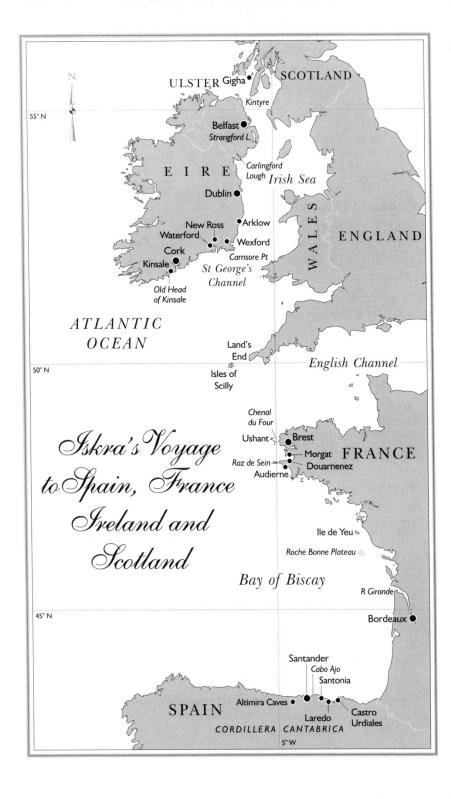

N

SCOTLAND

ULSTER Gigha

Kintyre

55° N

Belfast
Strangford L.

E I R E

Carlingford
Lough *Irish Sea*

Dublin

New Ross Arklow
Waterford
Cork Wexford
Kinsale Carnsore Pt
St George's
Channel

WALES

ENGLAND

Old Head
of Kinsale

*ATLANTIC
OCEAN*

Land's
End

50° N *English Channel*

Isles of
Scilly

Chenal
du Four

*Iskra's Voyage
to Spain, France
Ireland and
Scotland*

Ushant Brest

Morgat FRANCE
Raz de Sein Douarnenez
Audierne

Ile de Yeu

Roche Bonne Plateau

Bay of Biscay

R Gironde

45° N

Bordeaux

Santander
Cabo Ajo
Santonia

Altimira Caves Castro
Laredo Urdiales

SPAIN

CORDILLERA CANTABRICA

5° W

beach of El Sardinero, deserted now in the late evening. Soon
we rounded Punta del Caballo, inside the island of Santa
Maria, looking like a child's birthday cake and sailed into the
ample estuary on which the city of Santander is built. We
anchored close in by the yacht club, rowed ourselves ashore
and sat ourselves at a sidewalk table on the paseo that runs
beside the harbour with a bottle of vino and a tapa of fried
squid. We spent an hour in an exquisite reverie of the
preceding days and nights, our musings becoming more
euphoric as the bottle emptied itself. We rowed unsteadily on
board, the night silent, the stars gazing down, slept an
unbroken, untroubled sleep.

2

Biscay's Malice

Santander is much neglected by English cruising yachts – they tend to avoid the north coast of Spain. The anchorage off the yacht club, although convenient to the city centre, is made uncomfortable by the constant swell and the difficulty of landing and leaving the dinghy at the club steps. We found a happy alternative a mile down stream, a good beach tucked in behind the entrance to the bay at Magdalena. There is a restaurant where one can sit in comfort over an evening meal. The view across the bay merits a glance – mountains along the skyline reflecting the setting sun, the wide estuary, the rocky Punta del Caballo with its winking light, white sand, the darkening blue of the sea and *Iskra* in the middle ground swinging gently to her mooring. Here we found a free mooring and the friendly Youth Sailing Centre who gave us permission to use it. It was calm, the water blue and clean for swimming and the beach a pure white sand. We could catch a bus to the city centre or walk through a garden overlooking the estuary, or walk over the Magdalena Peninsula to Sardinero. This, we found, is a watering place made popular by Spanish royalty rather as Brighton was made popular.

During the cholera outbreak in France in 1849 Sardinero was considered a safe resort. Wealthy Madrileños and Parisians who were in the habit of spending the summer months in Biarritz, Wiesbaden, Bagnares and the resorts of the Côte d'Azur, flocked to it. Hotels were quickly built and an enterprising entrepreneur soon started a coach service between the resort and the centre of Santander. Soon it became possible to travel this route by steam train. The Spanish Queen, Isabel II, was advised by her doctors that a dip in the pure waters of the Mar Cantabrico would be the very thing for her herpes. She came to Santander, took over the Aduana, displacing the officers and seriously disrupting the customs service. Special furniture was ordered for her from Paris, there was non-stop entertainment and fiesta for the months of July and August. Every day the queen, accompanied by her husband and sons, made her way to the beach at Sardinero. The resort flourished from that day on and still flourishes, retaining its dignity and a certain Victorian, or perhaps Isabelian charm. Wendy and I would row ashore in the morning, leaving our rubber dinghy on the beach outside the restaurant in the care of one of the waiters. We would walk over the peninsula of Magdalena and down the hill to Sardinero where we would find our cup of morning café con leche, with a view across the beach and over the bay past Santa Maria to the wide waters of the Bay of Biscay.

There is a long, lonely beach across the estuary by ferry from Santander. The landing place – it is hardly a town or even an 'aldea', is called Somo. The beach is as beautiful as any I have seen, rivalling Bondi and Cocacabana and Varadero in Cuba, even beaches in the west of Ireland and Scotland. It is deserted except perhaps on a sunny Saturday or Sunday. We walked along it for miles, the sand clean and hard and springy, the air warm but crisp with the tang of the sea. The combers roll in from mid ocean in majestic procession, tumbling over themselves as the sand shoals towards the beach, releasing the pent-up energy stored behind their concave fronts in rolling salvoes, like an army in line of battle. I took off my clothes and waded out to meet them. It was a conceit. I was engulfed, drawn out by the under tow, picked up high and deposited breathless and frightened on the sand. Wendy dragged me to safety like a piece of flotsam.

Iskra needed a scrub. She had not been on the posts to have her bottom cleaned and painted since her lay-up the previous autumn and she was beginning to be sluggish. I had thought that we might be able to put her against the inner harbour wall in Santander and paint her at low tide but we

18

found that there was no room. "You must go up river Señor," the old waterman said to us, "to the yacht marina. They will haul you out and paint the bottom." It was a long way up river through pouring rain and a hard wind from the west. The marina was large and very expensive, a few Spanish yachts but most of them big German and French and English boats whose owners came and went by air. Spain is no longer a cheap country. It cost £200 to lift *Iskra* out and put her back in the water. The day was cold and drizzly. The people in the yard seemed surprised that we had the anti-fouling paint on board and intended to paint *Iskra* ourselves, but they offered no objection. This evidently was a brand of yachtsman they were not familiar with. When Wendy turned to in the old shirt and trousers she keeps for anti-fouling, they were amazed. We got the job finished in a day and sailed back down the river with a rejuvenated boat. She prances like a newly shorn lamb when her bottom has just been painted.

The caves of Altamira are in rolling green country a few miles from the ancient town of Santillana del Mar. We went from Santander by train to Torelavega, then bus, then a taxi from Santillana so that we could arrive in time for our appointment at 10 am. Only five people at a time are allowed in. The first person to see the painting of the great red ochre bison and the wonderful running deer was a bright nine-year-old called Maria. She was exploring the cave with her father Marcelino Sautuola when she strayed into the cavern which is now called the bison cavern. The floor of the cave was only two feet below the ceiling – the Palaeolithic artists of 15,000 years ago must have lain on their backs painting the roof close above their heads. Maria's father, something of an archaeologist and with a penchant for exploring caves, immediately recognised the importance of their find. By the light of an acetylene lantern they wormed their way round the cavern, identifying deer, boar, bison, horses, goat-like animals, human beings and arrows flying through the air. The cavern is big, the roof is close covered with the paintings. They are extraordinarily vivid and alive.

Now the floor has been dug out so that it is possible to walk round and see the paintings in comfort. The entrance is well hidden. It was first found by chance in 1868 when a hunter called Modesto Perez ran to rescue his dog, trapped by the leg in a rocky crevice. It was another eleven years before Maria found the paintings. The level drops steeply inside the cave entrance – there are still the remains of a fire and the bones of animals from prehistoric times. The caves are extensive, the animals are full of grace and movement, there is an air of hushed awe in the presence of things that are so old in the time scale humans apply to themselves. The paintings look as though they might have been created yesterday. What is remarkable is their extraordinary beauty, the consummate skill of their execution and the depth of expression they convey. The running deer, a creature of infinite grace some eight feet long, has that familiar quality of heart-stirring pathos that never fails to wrench Wendy's heartstrings.

The weather turned unpleasant when we were in Santander and never really recovered itself for the remainder of that unsettled summer of 1992. The day we left was cold and foggy, unusual for Spain, even the north of Spain where unbroken sunshine could never be guaranteed. We fetched along the coast to the east in a light southerly wind, the heavy swell, often to be found in or around the Bay of Biscay making the passage uncomfortable and slow. The swell is called locally, the Vaga del Mar – the rogue of the sea. Even with the engine running *Iskra* was stopped by these lumpy, uneven waves. As soon as she gathered her way she was brought up with a jolt by a wall of hard water, shaking what little wind there was out of the sails. In a galerna, the north-west gale which is a feature of this coast, the sea that kicks up over this swell is formidable.

This is bad weather for Wendy, sending her straight to her bunk where she lies more or less in misery depending on the violence of the motion. If the weather had been clear I would have found peace for her behind Cabo Ajo (Ajo is the Spanish word for garlic) where there is a shallow estuary opening into a long river. I have passed this place several times but have never found conditions good enough to attempt the entrance. This time it was pouring with rain and thick. When the Vaga del Mar is running, the swell breaks dangerously along this coast. As it was, Wendy had to wait until the afternoon when we rounded the bluff Monte Buciero marking the entrance to Santonia. We stopped short of the town, just inside the entrance to the Ria where we found a mooring off Laredo Yacht Club.

In fact the town of Santonia is a dismal place although it should be beautiful, tucked in behind the mountain in lovely surroundings. During the Civil War there was an ugly massacre of republican sympathisers by Franco's troops. Columbus's navigator and cartographer, Juan de la Cosa, came from the town and the Santa Maria was built here, or possibly at Colindres within the Ria. Laredo also has an ancient town, the 13th-Century Romanesque parish church on a pinnacle of rock high above the old city. It has all been swamped by holiday development which has covered the peninsula on which the town is built with concrete, peppered with high rise flats and hotels, all empty except for the summer months. The population of the town swells from a modest 10,000 to over 100,000 in July and August. The sewage system and infrastructure are geared to the winter, not the summer.

Castro Urdiales is no more than 12 miles from the Ria of Santonia. It is a fine man-made harbour contained behind two massive stone walls. The cathedral stands defiantly on high ground at the western end of the wall, above the old harbour, braving the north west galernas. The yacht club is right in the centre of the town and there was a free mooring immediately outside it. Castro was the Roman port of Flavio Briga. The sprawling cathedral, built within a web of flying buttresses, was started at the beginning of the 13th Century. It took 200 years to complete. The Meson Marinero, the best seafood restaurant on the coast, is in the ancient part of the town under the cathedral. I took Wendy there for a tapa of squid and pulpo as soon as we arrived. The yacht club turned out to be a most friendly, welcoming place; we were introduced to the president and soon became involved in a discussion about classic boats in the glass bar overlooking the harbour. Someone produced a copy of a yachting magazine with pictures of *Iskra* and we asked them all on board to look at her.

We stayed for a week, wandered about the town and the surrounding countryside with aimless, sensuous enjoyment, chatting to the locals, plying ourselves with seafood, allowing the days to slip by with smooth, contented ease, free of all constraint. One day we took a bus back along the spectacular coast road to the old town of Laredo, on another we walked for miles, across the main Bilbao road and into the countryside. We came to a village in a deep valley – a tiny place which seemed in some way to have escaped Spain's headlong rush into the present, retaining the charm of the old without its overtones of brutality. We walked along a back road across an old stone bridge over a fast-flowing, crystal stream. There were small stone-walled fields up the side of the mountain, new mown hay raked into cocks, the sweet smell of manure, ducks, geese, small, bright birds. Up the hill was a farmyard with a donkey cart and the conical maize stacks, common to the north and west of Spain; pears, apples and figs were growing everywhere. We passed a pony and trap. In the little bar the señora was delighted when Wendy noticed her garden. She gave us dark, country bread and anchovies and olives as a tapa with our wine. The bar was dim, shafts of sun between showers straining through narrow windows in the stone walls. There were a few locals, a new puppy, no sign now of the lounging, arrogant guardia who would have monopolised the bar a few years ago in Franco's time.

We enjoyed our few weeks in Spain in spite of the weather. We had found it easy to be happy in a country which has changed so much over the last few years and so obviously for the better. There has been a lifting of the spirit, the sudden freedom to talk, to discuss, to shout to the roof tops if need be.

Before, the oppressive eyes and ears of the regime were watching and listening in every corner. The past in Spain is quickly and thankfully forgotten.

Our week-long sojourn through a happy haze of idle enjoyment was shattered when we realised that if we were to be in Brest for the start of the festival we would have to leave Spain and make our way across Biscay without delay. It had been unseasonably cold and wet since our arrival, with some strong west and south-west winds, although Castro itself, protected to some extent by the curve of the coast and by its massive harbour wall, had been a haven of peace. With my usual optimism I reckoned that we would be happy enough with south-westerlies even if they did blow up a bit. The course from Castro is north, the wind would be on our quarter, a good wind for *Iskra*. In a strong blow on the quarter I would set the storm trys'l and she would be safe enough and fast enough even if a bit uncomfortable. Wendy would probably be sick for a day, or perhaps two days, but then she would get over it and begin to enjoy the voyage. It was mid summer, the chances were the sun would shine and it would be warm. Perhaps the winds would be light as a bonus for her. I went over the gear carefully, checking that *Iskra* had suffered no minor chafes or wear to shackle, wire or rope. I tightened the rigging screws, oiled the vane steering gear and made everything ready for sea. She was in reasonably good order. She was leaking a bit but she always leaked a bit and it was nothing that could not be taken care of by a few strokes of the pump.

I knew she needed the attention of David, or Ariane or another of the Maldon shipwrights. She could wait another few months until the winter. She had been promised a re-fit, last year and the year before. This winter she would really get it. We would go on Saturday morning. It would be nice if it would stop raining but once clear of the coast, I reckoned, everything would be fine and settled. Usually if we go to sea when the weather is not at its best, it improves once we gain the open ocean and settle down to the voyage. There was fiesta in Castro on Friday night. Fireworks and singing in the streets until the small hours, the music amplified by huge loudspeakers to make certain that no one was excluded from the general goodwill – whether he liked it or not. We visited the Mesun Marinero and feasted on pulpo and perceves and mejillones for the last time, tumbled into bed to get what sleep we could through the noise.

It was bright and fine when we left early the next day, a morning breeze from the south. We had said goodbye to our friends in the yacht club and to the waiter in the Mesun Marinero. The forecast wasn't good but it wasn't bad – a fresh westerly wind. We hoisted sail before leaving the harbour; main, the working jib and the big reaching stays'l. I set up the bobstay under the bowsprit, swigging it up good and hard on the tackle and then we let go the mooring and pointed *Iskra* to the harbour entrance. As we got clear the breeze took us, heeling us and wafting us gently out between the massive harbour walls.

We looked back at the town, still asleep after its excesses of the night, the early sun throwing long shadows over red roofs, tree lined avenues and squares, the deserted promenade round the harbour's edge. There was no movement, no sign that the town lived and throbbed, only the lighthouse up beside the cathedral gave winking evidence of life after fiesta. As the town spread up the mountain behind the close jumble of roofs and alleys and narrow cuts around the harbour it thinned itself, became spacious and dignified with big tiled mansions, ample gardens and tall trees. There must be people up there, Wendy thought, waking up, rubbing their drowsy eyes, drawing breath for the new day, gazing out of their windows at the town and the placid harbour spread before them. Perhaps there was one soul to spare a thought for the small brown patch of sail making its way out into the wide ocean. The notion gave her some comfort.

The wind soon went from south to west. We were able to point the course with a few degrees to spare, the sheets nicely started. Soon *Iskra* felt the Bay of Biscay slop, a distinct

pattern and configuration of waves that seems to be peculiar
to the Bay. Different oceans, even different parts of the same
ocean have their own distinctive wave patterns. The North
Sea is different from the Irish Sea, both are different from the
English Channel, the Thames Estuary is different again.
Waves born and nurtured in the spaces of the ocean are of
another order again, their progress ponderous, leisurely,
benign until they are roused by the power of wind. Then they
become wonderful to behold from a small boat. They embody
a majesty, an absolute power, remote and fearful. Waves in
shallower, narrower waters, smaller and more volatile than
their sisters, are nonetheless deserving of respect. Being
shorter and steeper they have a quality of vicious malevolence
that is seldom seen in the ocean. They do their mischief in
sudden, evil bursts of energy, they wear and worry and tease,
like rats, leap up at you suddenly and unexpectedly, wear your
spirit with persistence and cunning.

The Bay of Biscay is something between the two. When the
wind blows it takes to itself the worst aspects of both. The
waves are big like ocean waves because they come unimpeded
over 2,000 miles and they are steep like estuary waves because
of the continental shelf and the uneven bottom they find
when they reach it. They have a peculiar twist to them that
imparts to a yacht a uniquely uncomfortable motion. *Iskra*
began to dance to their tune. The wind went to the north-west
and increased. A thin line of bilge water had appeared along
the lee side of the cabin sole. "It must be the topsides," I
muttered as I pumped her dry, "too much strong Spanish
sun."

I had to reef – it was urgent. The wind came in sudden
puffs, one laid on top of the next so that in a few minutes it
was blowing force 5 or 6. As I climbed into my oilskins I could
see that Wendy was already sick. I could do nothing to help
her. The motion was appalling, *Iskra* hurling herself about
like a demented creature. First I changed the big stays'l for
the working sail – an unpleasant job in a rough, head sea. The
sail must be unhanked from the forestay so that you must

crouch in the very eyes of the ship, haul the sail down the stay, fold it as best you can, and bring it aft. Then the smaller sail must be set in its place. Even hove-to, *Iskra* was plunging her bow into the waves so that they slopped over the foredeck in heaps of cold water. I put two reefs in the main, working slowly and methodically to a routine I have perfected over the years. She was steadier and safer with the reefs tied in but now the wind had backed another point to north-north-west. Close hauled and hard on the wind she would no longer point the course.

I brought my wet self and a bundle of wet sails into the cabin, stuffed the stays'l away in the fo'c'sle. Wendy was sitting on the lee bunk, a picture of misery, her bucket hanging in its place on the stove, already the recipient of a swill of noxious bile. The bilge water was over the cabin floor again, the same thin line along the lee side. She was leaking, it could no longer be denied. Then I in turn was attacked – by a sudden and immediate diarrhoea. The pulpo of the Mesun Marinero was paying me back. Wendy refused to lie down on the lee bunk which is the most comfortable. In the lee bunk you are cradled in the curve of the ship, in the weather bunk you must be held in with a canvas bunk board to prevent you from being hurled out. "You must have it," she said, "you'll sleep better and you'll get more rest. It doesn't matter about me – I'm useless anyway until this stops." In fact she is never useless however ill she may be. She found me some tummy medicine in the first-aid.

By evening the wind had increased again. *Iskra* was sailing quite fast, even in the confused sea, steered by her Aries vane with its usual competence and good temper. I have had the vane for as long as I have had the boat; it gives unending service, demands little except a drop of oil from time to time when I think of it. *Iskra* is heavy enough to be able to shoulder her way through the waves in a strong wind but it is a wet, uncomfortable business, not like the easy, fair wind motion of the passage out across the Bay. With the wind fair you can drive a boat, pile on sail, sit back and watch her while she does

Out and across the Bay from Castro Urdiales.

Soon it was rough and unpleasant.

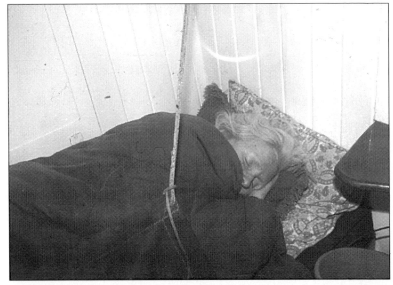

Misery.

The cabin is spacious, with standing headroom.

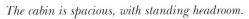

the work. Sailing downwind is the gentleman's way. Against the wind is another tale. Now *Iskra* is master, she dictates the pace and the direction of her progress. Now she cannot be driven, only coaxed and persuaded to her business. She has more stamina, more stomach for punishment than we have. She can plough through the ocean for day on day, hurling herself at the waves, smiting them with sickening jolts, sending green water rolling across her foredeck to hit the coach roof in a smother of foam, shaking herself until you believe her fastenings will start. I'm the one who gives in, not *Iskra*. As she smashes herself painfully to windward I throw in the towel, tiring of the discomfort. "I'll tuck in another reef," I muttered, "she's labouring."

I pumped her again, it was ten minutes before the pump sucked dry, buckled on my safety harness. Wendy was in her bunk, tied in like a Christmas parcel, her cheeks pale, an old brown blanket tucked round her back, woolly slippers. She wrote in her log for that day, "I just want to be at home in my garden and away from this horrible place. I hate it."

I emptied her bucket, gave her a weak kiss. "I'm going up to reef again – I won't be long – she'll be easier. The wind may drop when night comes." We both knew it wouldn't. I pumped again. "This is a bad business," I thought to myself, "I only pumped her a few minutes ago." I worried about the leak as I put in the third reef. I found it hard to credit. She had been straining for a few hours but it was nothing she hadn't gone through before. I couldn't believe, or I didn't want to believe that it was anything serious. It must be a seacock – the lavatory perhaps. With the third reef she was easier and easier to live with. The worst of the crashes went, her progress was slower but more tolerable. I checked carefully round the deck but found nothing amiss. She would do for the night.

The night slid a blanket of darkness under grey skies, no hint of moon or stars, only a faint, diffused shimmer of light over the restless waves. I lit the oil navigation lights, set them up on the coach roof and the stern – better than using the batteries. They shed a soft pool of red and green over the waves, somehow reassuring in the blackness of the night. They save the batteries for the electric pump. The bilge water was over the floor again when I went into the cabin. The cabin lamp cast its rich light over Wendy's sleeping form. Sleep would make her better sooner and surer than any potion or palliative I could devise for her. I would make her a honey and ginger drink in the morning – perhaps a lightly boiled egg. I checked the seacocks, checked as much of the yacht's planking as I could see through the lockers – nothing amiss. I was hungry, I was getting tired, I would have to sleep soon. I know it is essential to keep myself rested. Wendy had left me a stew, ready in a glass jar, a delicious thing, all seasoned with herbs and garlic. I watched the saucepan on the gimballed stove swinging itself back and forth with the motion, sniffed the aroma of goodness. Before the stew was hot the bilge needed pumping again. Something was very wrong.

I ate my stew. It made me warm inside, looked around at the darkness of the night. *Iskra* flogged on, throwing aside the lumpy seas, rearing and plunging still but with a lesser violence. She seemed to leak less when the roller jib was furled and her speed reduced. "She must be straining somewhere," I thought. There was no light to be seen save our own navigation lights, nothing to relieve the ocean's dark boundaries. I ought to turn her and go back – pumping every half an hour was not a sensible option – I wouldn't be able to sleep and I would exhaust myself. We had come 50 miles out into the Bay according to the log, with another 250 miles to go to the Raz de Sein. We were being forced off our course to the east, towards the long, featureless and inhospitable coast of Les Landes, in the neighbourhood of Bordeaux. If the wind continued to head us we would have to tack off-shore, increasing the distance.

I hadn't said anything to Wendy about the leak but I guessed she had seen or heard the pump. She would know from my manner that something was wrong. I knew she wouldn't say anything – she would leave it to me. She has an unswerving faith in my judgement on these matters, not always justified perhaps, which has always carried her through the adventures we have suffered together. I pumped again and then I lay down in my bunk to rest and to think. Without the jib, *Iskra* would probably go for an hour.

I still couldn't believe she had sprung a leak. I know she's old but I know that she's strong and sound – except for the starboard side where a couple of her steamed ribs are cracked. David and I had looked at her carefully – he had warned me about the starboard side but not with the degree of urgency he reserves for jobs that must be done without delay. A good look in the turn of the bilge under my bunk before it got dark had revealed nothing. Seacocks, galley drains, propeller shaft, engine cooling water were all tight – I had looked at them as well. Then I thought back to hauling out in the travel lift in Santander. I had looked round her carefully – the only doubt I remember was in the bolt through the stem that carries the bobstay. We had trouble with this bolt in the West Indies and had replaced it. My mind was going like a steam engine, images flashing in and out of it. Deep inside, I had the feeling that if I persisted, if I went through everything I had done to her or observed in her or not done to her or thought about her over the past few weeks I would find the answer. And then slowly and almost deliberately the answer came to me and I knew that I had it. The bobstay, that was it, the bobstay.

Iskra's bobstay is a length of chain running from a bolt through the stem, just at the water-line, to the bowsprit end. Its purpose is to steady the bowsprit, to prevent it from being forced upwards by the pull of the jib in a strong wind. The chain has a two-fold purchase in the top of it so that it can be hauled tight from the deck when we go to sea and slacked off in harbour to keep the stay out of the way of the anchor chain or the mooring rope. When we left Castro I had hauled the tackle good and tight – I remembered sweating it up until it was bar tight. But of course the pull of the stay, which would be a very strong pull in a hard wind, is at right angles to the bolt through the stem, subjecting it to a heavy sideways strain.

As *Iskra* lifts and falls in the seas the bobstay would take the weight of the whole rig. The bolt must have moved a fraction, allowing water to come up beside it. It was the bolt that had given trouble before.

I got up, grabbed a torch and went into the fo'c'sle, up into the bow where all the spare gear is stowed. It is all neatly packed right up in the eyes of the ship – racks with spare rope and spare tackles and sails and all manner of things which I have never used in anger but which I continue to carry on board from year to year. Sheets of copper for repairs to the hull, a large sheet of lead for an emergency repair, the anchor weights, spare canvas, twine, boxes of bolts and screws, oil lamps, marine glue, caulking cotton, hemp and marlin, spare blocks, a grapnel, all share the cramped, triangular space as far forward as it is possible to go. The whole lot leaps in the air as *Iskra* climbs the face of a wave, then plunges down with a noise like a drum roll. I excavated down, moving aside the piles of gear until I came to the stem itself. I shone the torch – there was the bolt, its big washered nut proud of the timber.

Each time *Iskra* dived a spurt of water forced its way past the washer and ran away into the bilge – enough to fill a bucket in a minute, I reckoned. I came out of the fo'c'sle, leaving the rubble of my excavation strewn about. I glanced at Wendy, her eyes closed, apparently asleep. I climbed back into my oilskins and harness, worked my way for'ard from hold to hold up the deck, found the bobstay tackle where it is made up on a cleat by the bowsprit. I eased it back. It gave a little jump as I took the turns off the cleat. Clearly it had been under strain. I went back inside and looked for'ard again. The water had stopped. Wendy opened a bleary eye. "It was the bobstay bolt – I fixed it." I don't think she minded – she was past minding. All she wanted from life was a calm day. I slept like a baby for an hour, then got up and looked around the horizon, then slept for another hour. *Iskra* had stopped leaking.

The wind freshened again, the seas increased, her motion more violent. It blew hard from the north all day Sunday and all Sunday night, became not gale force but a strong, wearing wind, force 6 with an occasional, stronger gust. I believe it was the most unpleasant spell of sailing I have ever experienced – certainly Wendy had never been more miserable or for as long. We made slow progress through the head seas, gradually being pushed further and further to the east so that by Monday morning we were close to the Roche Bonne Plateau, a shallow place where I knew the sea would be exceptionally rough. At noon the sun made a fleeting appearance and I was able to snatch a sight. It gave me a latitude to cross with a radio bearing of Ile de Yeu. I was pleased enough to have a firm position – the shallows were no more than a few miles over to starboard. I put *Iskra* about and stood out into the bay.

We had passed through some of the roughest water to be found all up and down the European seaboard. *Iskra* kept to her purpose with dogged persistence, never hesitating, never faltering in her stride. She made her way with uncanny certainty, like a good horse on a rough track, dodging and feinting to find a path through the best water. The waves had a vicious twist adding an extra dimension to her movement so that inside, it was impossible to stand for an instant without a firm handhold. They seemed to leap at her from all directions, bursting over the decks so suddenly that she would be assailed by a wall of water at her bow, another at the same moment rolling over her quarter. Sometimes they would jump up at her lee side, clawing and worrying at her and sometimes she would smite them head-on, shaking herself to a standstill, sending a column of spray high in the air and stinging over the deck. She was sailing as close to the wind as she would go without losing her way, with three reefs in the main and the working stays'l. When it eased, I broke out the jib and gave her extra speed. She responded to it at once, leaping ahead in great bounds of energy as she felt its pull. With the extra speed she tore through the seas like a mad dog, hurling herself forward with abandon, smashing and flaying her way through an army of ferocious soldiers intent on holding her in check. I watched her, listened to her complaining creaks and groans, felt her anguish as she struggled against this overwhelming force and then I could bear it no longer. I hove the tripping line, eased the sheet and rolled the jib away to slow her down. The motion and the strain and the discomfort all lessened with her speed.

The cabin was a haven of peace after confusion outside. *Iskra*'s old wooden hull makes good noise insulation – once the hatch slams shut on the clamour of a rough sea, all is quiet and ordered below decks. The gimballed lamps, the compass, the galley stove all swing in unison with the ship's roll. The chart table is a solid base, I can wedge myself with one knee against the side of Wendy's bunk, one leg behind me, chocked beside the galley locker and be fixed in position with both hands free for chart dividers and the parallel rules. The navigation books and tables are held behind a wooden batten on the shelf in front of me. Everything is to hand – echo sounder, hand-bearing compass, the VHF radio fastened to the deckhead above, the radio direction finder in a neat rack. The dark mahogany and teak of the cabin is set off by white paint on the cabin sides, a few bright pictures, the polished brass lamps and the brass fog horn fastened to the bulkhead, the old copper charcoal stove to keep us warm and dry. The stove is enclosed and can be used at sea quite safely. When we sailed up the coast of South America in winter a few years ago we kept the stove alight through a southerly gale straight from the Antarctic. We were dry and warm until the wind dropped and the sun came up. At sea the smart carpet over the cabin sole is folded away and stowed in the fo'c'sle – everything moveable is put away and chocked off against the motion.

I know that I am master in my own domain, wherein lies much of the enchantment of sailing small boats. Even Wendy, who shares equally in everything I possess, recognises that *Iskra* is a part of my psyche. In the world ashore a man is often no more than a tiny unit of little consequence, his life submerged in the affairs of others. He spends his working hours in some conglomerate where his impact is miniscule, hardly to be noticed. The actions he takes in his daily round may contribute to the general scheme of things but in themselves they are meaningless. He comes home, pecks his wife on the cheek and sinks into the hierarchy of his family, submerged until another day brings him to the light.

Put the same man aboard a boat and that man becomes king. Suddenly, his word is law, his edict runs, his actions produce immediate and evident results. If he is wise, his expertise can at once be seen and appreciated by himself and those around him. A pretty manoeuvre, nicely carried out, produces general acclaim. If he acts foolishly, retribution is close at hand – there are no slick cover-ups or subtle evasions at sea, the laws of cause and effect lie close together. The safety and the well-being of his crew and his ship depend on him. His ship is his mirror to the world. What he is, she is – any seaman can see it at a glance.

Wendy was still in her bunk, still lying in a state of misery. She could keep nothing down, she had eaten nothing for two days, only an occasional drink of water. I had tried her with the honey drink but it had come straight up. In all our sailing she had never been through so much misery for so long. My distress at her condition was beginning to be overlaid by real worry and fright. She was becoming dehydrated – if it went on for much longer there could be lasting harm in it. She was utterly miserable. At best, after this nightmare voyage, she would refuse to come again – a serious jolt to our way of life.

I said, "There must be something you can take – something in the medicine locker – this is serious."

"All right – there is something – a Stemetil Suppository – but you'll have to give it to me, I don't think I can – per rectum." I gave it her, following the instructions on the packet carefully and she went straight to sleep.

I studied the chart. There was little in the way of comfort to be found on the French coast in the southern part of the bay, a long, featureless wilderness of sand with no safe harbours south of the Gironde. Further north it was little better – Ile de Yeu was possible – I had never been there. Belle Isle is lovely with a good harbour but was so far to the north that we might just as well flog on to Audierne. On Monday evening the weather began to look finer, the wind slowly eased, a watery sun turned itself, reluctantly, into a fine sunset. "Its getting better – I'll make you another drink." The honey and ginger mixed with boiling water in a mug, makes a lovely drink. I made her sit up with cushions behind her back. The sea had mercifully gone down, the drug had done its work. She drank it slowly, sip by sip and it stayed inside her.

Wendy slept sound and long on Monday night but she was weak and shaky on her feet when she tried to get up in the morning. When she is so ill, although she is in her bunk, she gets no real sleep. She lies with her eyes closed in a kind of coma but when the sickness at last goes away it leaves her exhausted. I gave her a boiled egg and some thin, rather stale brown bread with butter on it and sat her in the sun in the cockpit. She began to smile weakly. "I'm going home on the ferry from Brest," she announced. I said "Yes darling."

It is an unending wonder to me that Wendy continues to come on these voyages in spite of the purgatory she passes through. There are few more unpleasant or debilitating afflictions than sea-sickness. She believes it is caused as much by fright, or perhaps nervousness, as by the physical motion. We can be in harbour and the boat rolling in the swell enough to turn her inside out and she will be quite unconcerned. The moment I say "Right we're going to sea," and start heaving the anchor chain, she begins to feel unwell. Strangely, I have never known her to show real fear, even in nasty situations – on the contrary she is invariably cool and level-headed when the chips are down. Equally, she is sometimes nervous and makes a fuss about small matters of little consequence. She is aware of the swings and roundabouts of sailing; she knows that when things are bad they will surely get better. At the same time her natural buoyancy stops her from fearing that when things are good they are certain to get worse. Deep inside herself she strikes a balance, reckoning the halcyon days and starlit nights, the rich encounters with the creatures of the ocean, as of greater value to her than the days of misery are a torture. Give her a spell at home and she will soon begin to yearn for the excitement of another voyage.

There was little wind on Tuesday, what there was of it from the north and north-east. It was slow, tedious going for little gain, always looking for any advantage to be found in a shift of the fickle wind, tacking again when it changed back. It was frustrating, needling weather, designed to fray the nerves and shorten the temper. I wrote in my log, 'swore at Wendy for not adjusting the vane properly – horrible of me. She was sick, tired, empty of food and feeling like hell and I swore at her. Could have bitten off my tongue. She wept and was miserable – but being Wendy, only for a minute. She is one for coming up smiling.' We ran the engine on and off during the day, more to keep up our spirits than for the distance gained. The lumpy sea was still with us, no longer a rough sea but enough to slow *Iskra* down. On Wednesday morning we came up with Point de Penmarche and at lunchtime we were tied to a mooring in the river of Audierne. We were pleased enough to be in harbour for a spell.

3

Change of Plan

The Classic Boat Rally in Brest was remarkable – an expression of corporate enthusiasm on a huge scale. There were hundreds, perhaps thousands of boats, of all sizes, all ages, all shapes, all rigs. There were dancers, actors, singers, musicians of every kind, craftsmen, acrobats, magicians. Somehow, by a miracle of organisation, they were all brought together in a week's jamboree split between the naval harbour of Brest and the nearby port of Douarnenez. The whole of France gave the rally its unqualified support; it seemed as if the whole of France packed itself into the two towns to take part in it. The city of Brest was cordoned off at every road – everyone who came to the rally paid ten francs to get into the city. They filled the quay side in a solid mass of smiling, good-natured citizens, they spilled over onto every boat alongside the harbour walls, they filled every bar, every restaurant, every aperture or nook which would accommodate a group of singers or clowns or raconteurs to entertain them. There were ships of all nations and all descriptions, each one crowded with visitors the whole day long. At times the quay was so dense with people that it was difficult to get ashore and force a way through.

When we arrived we were allocated a berth and given a bottle of red wine each, tins of biscuits, the festival programme. Everyone was good tempered, courteous and brimming with goodwill. We arrived the day before the official opening and already the harbour was stacked with boats, the town overflowing with visitors. We soon found friends; it seemed that everyone in the world was there. My son Adrian was there as skipper of a Thames barge, there were nephews, nieces, cousins, David was there in his own boat and

Ariane, together with a dozen other shipwrights from the east coast of England. We found friends from Essex, friends from America, from Australia, even from Iceland who had been drawn inexorably into this astonishing festival. The investment and the preparation must have been formidable. Every little sea port in France that had once given its name to a type of work boat, had managed to produce one example, either a restoration or a new build to the old design. There were a dozen square-rigged ships, innumerable fishing boats with all manner of strange rigs, replicas of Columbus's caravelles, a Ukrainian galley, Essex smacks, Thames barges, yachts, launches, canoes, steam pinnaces. On one breezy day we took part in a race of classic gaff cutters, which we won. We were given a prize – three bottles of good wine in a nice wooden case. The whole fleet of yachts and ships and launches and boats sailed in procession from Brest to Douarnenez, some twenty miles across the bay. It was a sight such as I have never seen before and am unlikely to see again. Ships, yachts and boats were spread from horizon to horizon, a kaleidoscope of colour and shape and size.

Douarnenez was less traumatic than Brest, the crowds not quite so dense, the noise and crush less pronounced, the organisation less efficient. We tied to a mooring buoy in the harbour, within half an hour three other large, classic boats were tied alongside us. While we were ashore a breeze of wind came and the mooring broke. *Iskra* ran alongside some obstruction, we do not know what, gouged a piece out of her topsides and wrenched off a chain plate. We were told she was taken in tow by a police boat. They used the main sheet to tow her, wrenching one of the cleats out of the deck. We found her tied forlornly alongside an old Motor Fishing Vessel . She had already been damaged in Brest when another boat ran alongside her while we were ashore, lifting the toerail and splitting the top sides. We needed somewhere peaceful and quiet where we could draw ourselves together, repair the damage and get ready to continue our voyage.

We are always attracted by jamborees such as the Brest

Classic Boat festival but when we go to them we soon tire of the crowds and the confusion. They are fine for a day or so, meeting old friends, parties in other boats, the jovial pleasure of shared experiences. We like exploring new places, wandering round the back streets, pottering into bars and cheap cafés, jaunts into the surrounding countryside by bus. In Brest we were aboard all manner of boats and ships; friends and acquaintances came on board *Iskra* in droves. It was a delight but we soon began to long for peace and quiet. The weather was unpleasant, there was too much of everything, too much noise, too many people. It wore us down.

After a few days in Douarnenez the festival began to peter out and life became calmer and more conducive to repairing the damage to *Iskra*. Adrian and all the barges set off for home, the lovely French fishing boats dispersed themselves up and down the Brittany coast and further afield. I made a good repair to the top sides for'ard with patent filler and a less good, but serviceable repair to the lifted toerail. I glued the old main sheet cleat together and fastened it back in the deck, took out the bobstay bolt that had troubled us in the Bay, repacked it and fastened it back in place. A coat of paint and a lick of varnish here and there had *Iskra* looking smart and neat. Douarnenez was a pleasant enough town when the crowds had thinned and ordinary life resumed. Like many small towns the place is spoilt by motor cars. They lie about all over the streets, even on the pavements; they clutter the main square, robbing it of its green, shady charm, making of it a dump for old iron. There is no inch of town that is not occupied by a car. They pollute, they make an unpleasant noise, they are not beautiful. Shakespeare wrote, "All this the world well knows, but none knows well to cease the heaven that leads men to this hell." He was talking about sex – it applies as well to cars.

It was on our way across the Bay of Douarnenez to Morgat that the idea of sailing to Scotland first took shape. It was a dull day, cold for the time of year and the wind was ahead, as it had been consistently since we had left Castro. With the rising glass the signs were that it would stay in the north-east, giving us a long, rough beat up channel to home if it held its direction. "Sometimes these high pressures stick for weeks and we will have to flog against it just like the Bay. Let's go to Scotland instead, we'd have a fair wind." Over a glass of wine in the little cafe in Morgat it began to look like a good idea. My nephew Richard lives in Connel, near Oban. He runs a charter yacht from the marina at Croabh Haven a few miles south of Oban. We could leave *Iskra* there for the winter, go home and come back in the spring to sail around the west coast of Scotland. "At the end of next summer we could sail her back to Essex, round the north or through the Caledonian Canal – what a trip!"

The idea put new life into the voyage. A new project – we could go to Ireland again, visit Wendy's relations and all our friends, sail up the east coast to Wicklow, Arklow, Howth and a dozen little places we had never been to. Next year we would have the whole of the west coast of Scotland to explore, one of the most beautiful cruising grounds in the world, then potter back to the east coast at our leisure. I telephoned Richard – yes, he would arrange with the marina to lift *Iskra* out for the winter, we could stay with him and Mary in Connel while we fitted out next year. "We'll be there by the end of August, give or take a day or so," I told him. I telephoned Adrian when he reached home. Yes, he would parcel up the winter cover from the shed at the top of the garden and despatch it to Croabh Haven. It was a splendid plan, he thought.

We left Morgat at five in the morning, sailed round Cape de la Chevre and across the wide entrance to the Goulet de Brest, close round Point de St. Mathieu to a little place called Le Conquet – my friend Johnny had recommended it.

Le Conquet is at the southern end of the Chenal du Four where the tide rips with great force between the mainland of France and a plethora of rocks and small islands out to Ushant, the westernmost point of France. It is a dangerous place. The tide takes a yacht so fast that it is easy to become confused, even lost among the shoals and rocks and swirling eddies. With wind against tide it is a very rough place. We motored into Le Conquet only barely in time. Another ten minutes and the tide would have set against us, making progress impossible with a light head wind and *Iskra*'s weak engine. There is a small anchorage among the rocks under the lighthouse on Point de St. Mathieu where I once spent a foul tide but it is a tenuous place, open to any westerly wind.

Seeing us hesitate inside the entrance, unsure of where to berth, a man in a dinghy rowed over to help us. "You may pick up that mooring monsieur – it is a good strong one and you will have water at low tide." People in France are refreshingly helpful and polite. We were never asked to pay, except that sometimes in a marina berth there would be a small charge. The whole of the Brest '92 Rally was without charge, both in Brest and Douarnenez. All very different from the south coast of England where sailing has become an exclusive pastime for moneyed people. There is no longer room for the impecunious boater, with a fine old vessel he has resurrected from some muddy creek, scraping together his pennies, spending his leisure hours painting and repairing and making do to keep his pride afloat. These characters have done much to make sailing irresistibly attractive but they are being driven out by managers and harbour masters intent on extracting from the boating fraternity every penny they can squeeze.

In Le Conquet it was possible to escape the cars by scurrying into the main square where all traffic was banned for market day. The square was packed with stalls where every conceivable thing to eat was to be found. Peasant women were selling their produce, there were cheeses from all over Brittany, large, florid men with berets and scarves and ruddy faces brought their crab and lobster and squid to the market. There were materials of every colour and quality, the coarse shirts and trousers worn by peasants. Tall, angular men with watch chains and dapper shoes sold toys and games and tricks, the bars were full of laughing, arguing traders and customers. The French are at their best on market day. We bought fresh sardines for supper, artichokes, asparagus. When the sun came out, briefly, we went for a walk along the cliff top overlooking the tumble and pother of the Chenal du Four, spotted and took note of the rocks we would have to swerve our way through in the morning. We ate ice cream dangling our legs over the harbour wall, drank a last glass of vin ordinaire in the quayside café.

"Here's to a smooth passage," I toasted.

"Amen," Wendy replied with a wistful smile. We rowed on board, made ready for sea in the morning. We were bound for Kinsale in the south of Ireland.

We were up and away early on Friday morning, a grey, windless morning with a light mist. We chugged out into the current already running fast to the north. *Iskra* was taken in charge by it at once. It swept us past Point de Kermorvan inside the tower on Grande Vinotiere and away towards Les Platresses, five miles to the north. I reckoned the tide at 5 knots, our engine giving us another 2½ knots. The mist was thicker outside, we soon lost the shore and all marks. I was looking for the buoy on Taboga, a nasty rock on our starboard side but we never saw it. Neither did we see the buoy off the Bas de Corsen which would have given us a lead past the Platresses. We chugged on through the damp morning, Wendy steering with all her concentration. We listened, we strove vainly to pierce the mist with our eyes. We saw nothing, heard nothing. Slowly the tension lifted. "We must be through it," I said, "if we were going to hit a rock we would have hit it by now." After an hour a breeze came from the north, *Iskra* began to sail close hauled – not very fast and not on the course but we were clear and safe.

With the wind came a short, rough sea, giving an unpleasant motion, not as rough as Biscay but enough to drive Wendy to her bunk almost at once. There was nothing for it but to tuck her up, fasten the bunk board and keep her warm.

Before this voyage, she had always come through the sickness after a day or two at most. This time it seemed to persist until we made harbour or the weather calmed. On the leg from Spain it didn't calm until the last day – I hoped it

Brest was solid with people.

Bright sunshine – at last.

Kinsale – a most peaceful harbour.

would this time. We managed to clear the French coast during the day and the night but it was tedious going with the wind, what there was of it, from the north. Well, I thought, it was this foul wind that made us decide to go to Ireland. Soon, when it goes to the north-east we will be able to free the sheets and skim off with it fair on the quarter, the motion will ease and Wendy will come to life. Then the wind changed – but not to the east. It went to the south west – a depression was coming in.

It was the dawn on Saturday that brought the new wind. The barometer began to go down but it didn't look like the depression that would bring a gale. The sky was hard but not unkind. Soon *Iskra* was bowling along, the log spinning nicely. By breakfast time I was putting two reefs in the mains'l, changing to the small stays'l. It was rougher now, spray driving across the deck but she was steadier with a good wind to hold her down. We soon passed across the shipping lanes and by lunchtime I was taking bearings of Land's End and the Scillies. She wasn't leaking over much, no more than the slowly increasing leaks that had been apparent for the last two or three seasons. My worry was for Wendy, not for *Iskra*. We could go into the Scillies and wait for a finer day; it would only postpone the trauma for her. Before we passed the Scillies I called Land's End radio and asked for a weather forecast. It was a repeat of what we had heard on the BBC – west to south – west, five or six.

"Would you like to go in to St Mary's?," I asked her. "We could quite easily – now before it gets dark. We could probably fetch it close hauled."

"No, we might as well go on, get it over with in one go – it won't make any difference, this voyage is fated anyway," and she turned over and buried her face in the pillow. By nightfall we were past the Scillies and headed for Ireland, a hundred and fifty miles to the north-west. I went sound asleep on the lee bunk for an hour, woke and looked around the horizon then slept for another hour.

The shipping forecast at midnight gave gales for Fastnet

and Lundy – we were in the middle of it. I tapped the glass it was 1021 millibars and steady, the wind had eased if anything – it wasn't much more than Force 5. "It's not a low glass, it isn't dropping, there are no nasty looking clouds, just overcast – I don't believe them." It's hard not to believe a gale warning but they are often false, or the gale is in an adjacent sea area or even the other end of the area you are in. "I'll put in another reef – just in case." *Iskra* was sailing quite happily, the seas were longer and easier and Wendy was showing signs of improvement. I put in the third reef, resentfully bowing to established wisdom although common sense told me it was mistaken. "Oh well, better safe . . ." Wendy said. I gave her a honey drink – it stayed down.

Things were looking up. There was no gale and no further mention of it from the pundits. In the morning I shook out first the third reef and then the second so that *Iskra* sailed nicely, the sheets just free, comfortably on the course. A limp sun came out for the first time in days, cheering us with promise of finer times. I picked up the radio signal from the Old Head of Kinsale, happily on the bow, put on a Mozart symphony, filling the boat and the spaces of the sea with sparkling logic.

Wendy ate a boiled egg. The sailing pendulum swung our way, driving off all discomfort, even the recollection of discomfort, allowing a serene contentment to lap round us. In the night we brought the lighthouse on the Old Head abeam, watched its even sweep skim across the dark waves. It was another moonless, cloud covered night.

I was tired, not much inclined to take *Iskra* into the harbour in the dark. "Why not heave-to and wait until morning?" Wendy suggested. "You can get some sleep – I'll watch her."

"Brilliant – a shaft of genius."

I pinned in the main sheet, drew the stays'l a'weather, rolled away the jib, set the tiller to lee'ard and she settled as easy and quiet as I could wish. Wendy had a bearing of the light to watch, *Iskra* was in a nice lee, hove-to on the off-shore tack. I slept for four hours, woke with the dawn. We sailed into Kinsale as the soft light brought to life a placid, smiling countryside – rolling wood and farmland, the sheltered estuary, ancient fortifications on either side of the narrow entrance, the sleepy town with yachts and a ship moored to its quays.

Behind the waterside Kinsale rises nobly up the hill, Georgian terraces and fine houses giving it grace and dignity. We spotted a mooring and tied to it. We have always enjoyed Kinsale, the last time we came to it from the Azores way out in the Atlantic. The town always vindicates our hope for a joyous landfall after days or weeks at sea. In Kinsale there is everything that is pleasant – a friendly yacht club, good restaurants, excellent pubs, easy shopping, a pretty, steep, winding town, glorious walks in the countryside around with sudden views of the estuary, *Iskra* peacefully swinging to her mooring. The mooring was for visitors – free of charge.

4

Fateful Passage

Wendy is an Irish Protestant. She was brought up on a farm in County Carlow, near the east coast harbours of Arklow and Wicklow. Her cousins still farm the land at Redcross in the foothills of the Wicklow mountains. Catholics and Protestants live side by side in the south of Ireland without friction, either religious or secular but the split in religion leads to a cultural split of which she is still aware. She went to a Protestant school and even now, there are schools that take only Protestant children. Robbie, who is married to Wendy's school friend Doris, is a teacher at one of the largest, in Dublin. The cultural split still goes deep. Protestants still tend to look towards England for political inspiration; they tend not to use the Irish language although this is compulsory learning in all schools.

We were having a cup of tea with the customs officer and his wife in Kinsale, old friends from previous voyages. She said, "Sure you should go to the Irish dancing tonight – in the Shanakee you'll find them." The pub was a warren of a place, low beams, smoky bars, a swarthy man in a cloth cap with an accordion, everyone dancing jigs and reels and singing lovely songs I had never heard, some wild, some sad, some jolly, in Gaelic and some in English. We were enthralled and wandered back to our dinghy glowing with pleasure. Wendy said, "This is something I missed when I was a child. I learnt all about Irish history and Irish culture in school but I never practised it – going to pubs or going to Irish dances was something girls from Protestant families just did not do. They still don't."

A week in Kinsale slipped by in a dream, this is the part of sailing that Wendy loves. Casual encounters – an American in a pretty little ketch, an Irishman waiting to sail round the world, a few boats we have met before. Walks over the hills behind the river and out to a country pub near the harbour entrance, along a white beach by the sea. We landed our bicycles and launched out into the countryside, exploring lanes and villages miles off the beaten track, Wendy ferreting out the history of the place and discovering its spirit. Doris and Robbie took us round the west of Ireland in their car, there were convivial dinner parties on board *Iskra*, the days evaporated. On a fine day we sailed round to Crosshaven to the Royal Cork yacht club. I had copies of three or four of my books on board which I sold to bookshops in Cork to help our finances. The Irish are the most literate people we have encountered, except perhaps the Icelanders – a writer is always welcomed.

The south-west wind blew hard while we were in Kinsale, with a lull the day we sailed to Cork, but there was wind again along the coast from Cork to Waterford harbour, a distance of some 60 miles – long Atlantic rollers topped by white capped seas, low cloud scurrying. *Iskra* was shortened down to three reefs in the main, her stays'l boomed out to take the following wind and to ease her steering. It would have been more comfortable with twins but the wind had been forecast for north-west, which would have been off the land and in calmer seas. Our chart showed a little place called Dunmore East at the entrance to the wide harbour of Waterford. We could see nothing of it, only the dark face of the sheer rock as we came hurtling along the coast with the gale behind us. Then Wendy saw the town high up behind a fold in the rock. "Look – in there, behind the point – it must be it." There was no sign of a harbour entrance. We gybed her, hauled the sheets and flew towards the land, lee rail under, seas sweeping over the deck. In a flurry of foam we ran under the lee of the cliffs and suddenly the harbour was there as we came round a corner of rock. All was calm and *Iskra* was among yachts and boats in an anchorage. We came slatting into the wind, dropped the main on the boom gallows and sidled up to a buoy, relieved and thankful to be in. It had been blowing a gale, we were told when we went ashore. A yacht had been wrecked across the harbour on the east side, three young men drowned. In the evening the wind died away.

We first met John Seymour when he came to give a lecture to our local society in Maldon. He is a prolific writer with books about Ireland, about farming and *The Complete Book of Self-Sufficiency*, a work from which we have derived much pleasure and much practical help. It tells how to do things, how to make things, how to live in the hinterland that exists behind the shallow fringe of modern society. "You must come and see us when next you sail to Ireland," he said. He lives by the side of the Barrow River which runs into Waterford harbour. A swing bridge carries the railway across the entrance to the river. We were advised to telephone the bridge master. "I'll open it for ye in the mornin'," he said, "at ten o'clock." We were up early and sailing up towards Waterford on a calm morning, as calm as it had been for a week. We soon came to the bridge with the young flood behind us. Punctually at ten o'clock we saw the bridge master at the big iron wheel and one span of the bridge swung open for us. He gave us a wave, "Ye can ring me when your comin' out."

The Barrow River winds itself through rural Ireland. At first prospect it is wide, serene countryside of farms, hedges, small fields, sweeping down to the river. There are trees along the skyline and in haphazard woods, reedy meadows by the water where birds pursue their untroubled lives, cattle peacefully grazing. As we twisted and doubled to follow the channel the river closed in, its banks steep, thick with oaks and elms, the woods climbing in clusters to the brow. We saw an Irish Hooker tied to the bank. "There she is – that's John's boat – we've arrived." We breasted alongside, tied *Iskra* fore and aft against the Hooker's black topsides. She was unconverted, scarred with the knocks and scrapes of her great age. "She must be 70 years old at least," John had told us. You could see her massive frames through the open hold, her mains'l loosely furled along the boom. John's house would be up the hill, hidden in the wood. We climbed a winding path through the trees. The house was open, there was no one at home.

We moved *Iskra*, anchored in the stream, letting out plenty of chain against the strongly flooding current, inflated our rubber dinghy. She would lie afloat in the stream at low water. It was beginning to blow again, the wind was already streaming through the tops of the trees. When we rowed ashore and climbed the path John and Angela had come back. They gave us home brewed beer, bread and cheese, country wine, an alcoholic and riotous lunch. We scrubbed ourselves in the luxury of a hot bath. "Come to dinner on board," we said. It blew harder in the afternoon, now there was a strong gale. I let *Iskra*'s anchor weight down the chain to steady her against the ebb tide which John told me might run at 6 knots or more after the heavy rain. Wendy spent what was left of the afternoon cooking. In the evening I rowed ashore with some difficulty, against the current and with the south-west wind screaming up the river.

John was waiting on the shore by himself – he is a big man, I was thankful Angela had decided to stay on dry land. I got him on board after a struggle, rowing up river out of the current for 150 yards before venturing into the stream. The tide took us like a missile down on *Iskra*. We both grabbed her rail as the dinghy tore past, clung on for our lives and carefully hauled ourselves on board. The table was set for dinner, a savoury smell wafted from the cabin, the oil lamps gave their warm light. Half way through the meal I felt *Iskra* tremble – I looked out through the cabin scuttle at the dark bank. It was sliding past. She was dragging fast. Dinner abandoned, John steered, the engine at full speed, Wendy and I at the anchor. We recovered it with a struggle and laid it again a mile upstream. She had brought up just before a right angled bend in the river. "In another three minutes," John said, "she would have driven ashore. This is a lucky ship." We were beginning to wonder how much luck we had left – we were needing it on this voyage. We kept John on board for the night, put him to bed in the fo'c'sle in the wee hours of the morning. I stayed up reading, dozing and keeping a lookout but *Iskra* didn't shift again. The next day the gale died and we sailed up this delightful river to New Ross, tied up outside the Mariner's Pub for our Guinness.

John Seymour took us to a tiny pub in Carrick on Saturday night, in the remote south-eastern corner of Ireland. It was hardly a pub at all, more a big room behind the village shop with a counter where the Guinness flowed. People drifted in, exchanged the pleasantries of the day, the news of the week, sat with a pint. Brindie produced a kind of large tambourine, or perhaps it was a drum, her husband a formidable mouth organ. Pat and Seamus both wielded accordions, another a banjo. They were well used to playing together, the music was full of sincerity and feeling. There were sad songs about emigration, about the potato famine, about poverty and unrequited love. Dominic was brilliant on a tin whistle; he contrived to play and sing at the same time. As the evening matured, the Guinness came and went, the music blossomed and swelled. John sang, rather badly, but it didn't matter. I delivered a narrative poem about the sea, also rather badly – I was a little drunk.

Then the Republican songs and poems got going; a song to the Unionists' tune of 'The Sash My Father Wore', suggesting that when Ian Paisley was hung by the sash his father wore, there might be peace. Brindie recited a poem about her late father's poteen – he offered a dram to St Peter and gained entry to the Pearly Gates.

Another westerly gale took us along the south coast of Ireland to Carnsore Point on the corner and then, at last, we were in the lee of the land, where the sea was smooth and the wind roared and whistled over our heads. The number of gales round our coasts is increasing year by year. Global warming seems to have had the effect of bringing the tracks of the Atlantic depressions further south, so that now, instead of spending themselves in the wide strait between Iceland and the Faeroes, they pass over Ireland and the west of England. I find from a 1960 Admiralty Pilot which I bought when I started cruising, that there were no summer gales in the Irish Sea in that year. In the summer of 1981 there were two and in 1992 we experienced four gales round the Irish coast. They have also increased in ferocity and in duration. All this makes sailing a more hazardous pastime. As global warming increases and as the measures needed to curb it are considered but not followed through, it is beginning to look as if the political system is failing. There is no sign that the squandering of the world's resources and global warming have any place on the political agenda. The Earth Summit in Rio in 1992 became an exhibition of complacency, its results to all intents and purposes nil. A few crank organisations such as Greenpeace and Friends of the Earth have an understanding of what is happening to the world. The likelihood is that the cranks are right and the politicians wrong. It is hard to believe that they can be unaware of the problems – like all of us, they are busy fiddling while Rome burns.

We doubled round the harbour of Rosslare, a bad place for a yacht we were told, to find a snug anchorage in the bay behind the town, working well inshore under a long beach with dunes behind and dropping our anchor on the pure, sandy bottom. The gale roared over our heads for the rest of the afternoon and for most of the night. Wexford, we decided to pass by. I believe it is a nice old seaport but the entrance is shallow and might be difficult with no good chart. Instead we spent an easy night hanging to our anchor and set off for Arklow early in the morning. It was a lovely sail on a windy, sunny day, close inshore past the smiling countryside, the same small fields, farms, woods rising to the Wicklow hills, the occasional Georgian house commanding a sweeping view over the farmland and the sea. The wind freshened again so that we were glad to gain the lee of Kilmaechel Point, stow sails and sweep into the narrow entrance to Arklow harbour. We found a berth in a quiet corner of the dock where there is an old, disused shipyard.

We spent two and a half weeks on this delightful and much neglected coast, sailing from one harbour to the next, making excursions on bicycles into the countryside, being taken for jaunts to Dublin by Doris and Robbie and staying a few days on the farm with Wendy's cousins. Ireland is a country we both feel at home in. The pace of life is less feverish than in England, there is still time to sit and talk and smile. Towards the end of August we were in Carlingford Loch, which is on the border between the north of Ireland and the south, the Mountains of Mourne over to starboard, farms and fields and hedges and woods to port and a newly constructed yacht marina. We came up to it just as the light was failing, found the entrance in the dark and felt our way to a vacant pontoon.

There were a number of yachts tied bow-on to the other side of the pontoon; the place clearly wasn't finished, no light at the entrance, no sign of life. We found the next day that it was really only half a marina "We'll be after finishing it in a while. We need to find a bit more money," the manager, Oscar, said. He was a relaxed, dreamy man. The western arm of the marina was finished with a good stone and concrete wall piled into the floor of the loch, but the eastern arm was no more than an old ship moored with heavy chains. There was another, smaller ship inside it with showers that were not quite working and a pleasant club house. We met Rowan Hart who asked us to give him an interview for his radio programme. It would help to move the books we had been selling to bookshops round the coast.

The Anchor Inn in the village was friendly, there were pleasant walks, an old castle, reputedly built by King John. The Mountains of Mourne on the other side of the bay sweep down to the sea as they are supposed to do, giving the place an element of romance and sentimentality which suited it nicely. In the evening the pub was crowded, there was more singing, this time with two guitars. It was midnight before we wandered off home.

We walked back to the marina through the rain with Rowan

Hart and another couple of revellers. As we got to the last hill overlooking the marina the rain became a deluge. It was coming up to high tide, the barometer was low – I had tapped the glass in the pub and it had jumped down. "When the rain comes before the wind, tops'l sheets and halyards mind," I muttered to Wendy. As I said it, the wind came out of the south-east; first a sudden gust which drove away the rain, then a stronger gust laid over the first and then the real wind. We ran down to the boat. She was lying alongside the pontoon, broadside to the wind. As it freshened a swell began to run in to the marina underneath the old ships. The pontoon and *Iskra* began to heave up and down. The wind was from the open Irish Sea blowing straight up the loch, the swells rolling unimpeded into the marina. We had out our biggest fenders but in half an hour *Iskra* and the pontoon were each hurling themselves up and down, *Iskra,* on the weather side of the pontoon, squeezing the fenders out from her starboard side. It was all Wendy and I could do to hold her off and push the fenders back into place.

The wind was a scream, it was impossible to stand on the pontoon, boats were crashing into each other all over the marina, people shouting for help, dark forms running in all directions. Wendy shouted, "We can use the dinghy seat." It was true, the dinghy seat was a fender – we had bought it in the West Indies because it was cheaper than a new dinghy seat. She found it under the cockpit floor, blew it up while I struggled to keep *Iskra* from smashing herself to pieces. It was a help but it wasn't enough. Then Rowan and two friends crawled out along the pontoon pushing a tractor tyre in front of them. "Tie it over the boom with a good rope," he shouted in my ear. I left them on the pontoon to fend off, went for a line and together we forced the tyre down between *Iskra* and the pontoon. "Sure it makes a darlin' fender," Rowan said. In an hour the tide began to go down, the worst of the wind blew itself out and the boats lay quiet. We surveyed the damage in the morning. Four boats were badly damaged, *Iskra* had several gashes in her topsides. We had been lucky – I was able to repair her. She was beginning to be battered by this voyage.

It was near the end of August. The unsettled, unpleasant weather that had been with us since we left Spain was getting worse – there were gales or strong winds and rain every few days. They were for the most part from the south-west or west so that we had calm seas on the east coast of Ireland. Sailing across Stranford Lough with our storm trys'l set we found ourselves in heavy over-falls. A big sea came curling aboard, lifted Wendy off the weather side of the cockpit and deposited her in a wet bundle on the lee side. She was fastened in by her harness.

As we turned to pass through the channel inside Copeland Island the wind swung round to the north-west giving us a hard beat to windward to the buoy off Orlock Point and for another eight miles across Belfast Lough to Carrickfergus. Only when we were within yards of the marina entrance, cold and wet and tired, did it occur to me that it was low water. I looked quickly at the almanac. Sure enough, Carrickfergus is a half-tide marina. With a curse, I put *Iskra* about, we let the sheets free and ran back five miles across Belfast Lough to Bangor.

My humiliation still had some distance to run. Taking in sail at Bangor, coming in to the marina, I got into a tangle with the mains'l, let the peak halyard go loose up the mast, passed the wrong side of a buoy. At last we tied alongside. I was ashamed, humbled, depressed, cold, wet, hungry.

"This is a terrible voyage," I said, "everything in the book has gone wrong."

"You'll feel better when you've had some supper."

It is 72 miles from Bangor to the island of Gigha on the west coast of the peninsula of Kintyre – as far as *Iskra* can sail in a day. Another, shorter day's sail, some 35 miles, would bring us to Croabh Haven from Gigha. It would all be done in two more days. Another way, perhaps a pleasanter way, would be to sail up the east side of the peninsula to Campbeltown, a mere 40 miles from Bangor, and then cruise easily through Kilbrannan Sound into Loch Fyne to

Lochgilphead and pass through the Crinnan Canal. This would take at least four days. It would be a leisurely voyage through the sheltered waters of the lochs with a dozen good anchorages and a selection of harbours where we could lie for a night – Dippen, Loch Ranza, Tarbert or at the entrance to Loch Gilp. The canal is only 6 miles long, we would work the gates ourselves. From Crinnan to Croabh Haven is no more than a morning's hop. It was getting late in the year, already early September and by this time we would both be pleased to get the voyage finished, *Iskra* tucked up safely under her cover for the winter and us snug at home. "We'll sail up to the Mull," I said, "when we get there we can decide which way to go."

The next day rained and it blew hard from the north-west, putting all thoughts of moving out of mind, but Bangor was no bad place to spend a day. The marina is one of the best we have seen, all new and lavishly finished, paid for, we were told, in part with EEC money. The staff were friendly and nice, we took luxurious showers. We put *Iskra* against a wall in a corner of the marina and gave her a scrub. "If we go straight to Gigha, we'll need all the speed we can get to make it in daylight." We would have to get there before dark. The little harbour at Gigha is not lit, I saw from the chart – there was a maze of rocks round the entrance, not a good place to be on a moonless night. Indeed, if we failed to get in we would have to sail on up the sound of Jura in the night, an equally unpleasant prospect. We would soon find ourselves in narrow, rock studded waters with strong tides and countless back eddies, none of it familiar, none of it well lit. The west coast of Scotland is a wild place, not to be trifled with.

The next morning was Saturday, September 5th – a day that is now engraved on my consciousness. We listened to the early forecast at 0600, it seemed possible. The north-west wind had dropped, the sky had cleared, the forecast spoke of moderate south-westerly winds during the first part of the day, slowly backing to the south-east and freshening. The day had a hard, brittle quality that boded no good. It was clear that more bad weather was to come. "I think we'd better go while we have the chance – otherwise we might be stuck here for days." Wendy agreed. "I really do want to get home," she said. We were out of the harbour by 0630, clutching cups of tea. The wind was light, westerly off the land, the sea calm. I put on all sail and *Iskra*, with her clean bottom, fetched across Belfast Loch at a good clip, past Larne and out into the North Channel. We had the tide with us, we would lose it somewhere off the Mull. Things were looking good. We had our breakfast sitting in the cockpit watching the green hills of Northern Ireland slide past. The wind began to ease as the morning spent itself. We started the engine to help her along. Soon we saw the Mull of Kintyre at the end of a finger of high green land pointing straight at us, the lighthouse a pimple on its western side. We were close to it after lunch. "We'll have to go to Campbeltown," I said, "with such a light wind we're not going nearly fast enough to make Gigha before dark."

"Oh well," Wendy said, "a pity but nothing for it." As I put her on course for Campbeltown the wind freshened from the south-east.

Suddenly she was sailing at her best speed, a fresh breeze, a calm sea, a clear sky, and a clean bottom. The barometer was falling rapidly. I made a quick calculation. Yes – at this speed we could be at Gigha before it got dark. We would have to sail at 6½ knots for four hours. The tide would soon be with us again, the south-east wind would be off the shore. It was forecast to freshen up to gale force but by that time we would be safely in. "We're going the other way," I said and brought *Iskra*'s bow round to skim up the west side of the Mull. For an hour we plugged the strong tide round the Mull, close to the shore off the village of Machrihanish, the steep, green shore of Kintyre slowly creeping past – a lonely place with a few scattered farms, sheep, stone walls, a land barren of trees. At 1800 the tide turned and *Iskra* began to move fast. It was one of the finest sails we have ever had. I steered, Wendy sat on the bridge deck, her feet dangling into the cabin. *Iskra* was inspired by speed – wind on the quarter, sheets free, sails pregnant with wind, the sea racing past, streaming along the lee scuppers. As I handed the tops'l to ease her, so the wind freshened again. She was sailing as fast as I have ever known her to sail.

There is an inherent thrill in speed which lifts the spirit, whether it is screaming round corners on a motor cycle, or a toboggan careering down the mountainside or a bicycle, the hedges whirring past in a dizzy green fizz, or in *Iskra* at 7 knots. At her best speed, she is very exciting – spindrift flying, wake bubbling, stays singing with strain, sails stiff, every part of her giving its all towards her onward progress. It isn't the speed, it's the means of it – *Iskra* at 7 knots is as thrilling as a high speed train. Speed tests every fibre of a boat. With the wind free, we can drive her as hard as her gear will stand – we are the masters of her. We watched her with a mixture of pride and apprehension, gauging the moment when we must shorten sail. Prudence would counsel now but we needed every ounce, every pinch of speed to get us in before dark. Soon we saw the island ahead and to port – low and long and thin, a scattering of rocks round its southern end. As the dusk slid into darkness we saw the lit buoy marking the Gigalom rocks to starboard, half a mile to the east of the island. "Now to spot the entrance," I muttered.

A squall of wind came sweeping across the strait, harbinger of the impending gale, heeling *Iskra* so that her lee deck was awash, forcing her to windward towards another group of rocks. Wendy could no longer steer her – it took us both with our weight behind the tiller to hold her to the course. "I must get the mains'l off her," I shouted and ran for the halyards, dropped the peak to spill wind from the sail. Just in time, she swung back on the course. "No time to reef properly – we'll have to leave her." With the mains'l scandalized Wendy could steer, her eyes glued to the compass. The channel was narrow – we could see the fading shape of Ailean Liath, a bleak rock, racing past the line of rocks to starboard. Now I peered out to lee'ard, striving to pierce the failing light to find the harbour. A wide bay opened out behind low rocks – no lights, no sign

Atlantic seas along the south coast of Ireland.

The tranquil Barrow River.

Storm trys'l off Stranford Lough.

Iskra at her best speed.

of a town, no sign of life. I reached in for the binoculars, swept them inch by inch across the line of rocks while Wendy steered, the scandalized mains'l flapping and banging. There should be an unlit red buoy at the end of them, marking the entrance. I would have to see it before we could go in – if not there would be nothing for it but to sail on and out into the sound of Jura.

Another inch and I came to the end of the rocks and then another. I caught a dim shape in the binoculars, it must be the buoy – a bit battered, paint weather-worn, looking as much like a rock as a buoy. But it must be it.

"I see it – it's there – port 20 degrees." Wendy was incredulous. "We're going straight for the rocks."

"No – the buoy's there – you're going straight for it – look at the compass. I'll roll up the jib, take the mains'l in."

I clawed the sail down – it was pressed against the mast and the stays by the wind but it came down, slowly, a mass of brown sail obscuring Wendy's view of everything except the compass. As I got the stays'l down the buoy slid past close to port. I could see the dark shape of a trawler lying to a mooring buoy – another mooring was beside it. I slung a tyer round the mains'l, cleared the mix of sail and ropes from over the side and started the engine. We brought her slowly up to the buoy, Wendy slipped a line through the ring and made fast.

It was calm in the little harbour, well protected from the south, the young gale driving over us. I squared up the deck, stowed the mains'l neatly with its tyers, coiled down the sheets, took in the vane from the self steering, checked the line on the buoy, pumped the bilge and looked round Ardminish Bay. There was one dim light from the tiny hamlet of Ardminish up the hill, the trawler beside us, no one on board. From what I could see of her, no one had been on board for a long time. I could make out a rock behind the trawler, the line of the shore curving round behind us. The harbour was open to the east – I could just see the Kintyre coast some five miles across the Sound. The mooring looked good, tucked in behind the point. One of the buoys laid for visitors by the Scottish Tourist

Board, I thought. I went below where Wendy was already busy with supper, its fragrance already filling the cabin with promise. The wind had shifted a little to the west of south, giving the anchorage a little more shelter. I could see pin-pricks of white surf breaking against the rocky shoreline. "We'll celebrate with the remains of last night's wine."

"That was quite a sail."

"Quite a sail," Wendy agreed. "I'm really happy to be in – it's bliss. I hope this mooring's good and strong."

I said, "We'll stay here until the weather moderates – probably the day after tomorrow."

Wendy said, "You ought to put another rope on the buoy – just to be safe."

I found a strong line among the spare gear in the fo'c'sle, "that'll hold her." I went for'ard, passed the line through the ring on the buoy and brought the two ends back to the bitts, one on either side of the bowsprit. The wind was gusting hard across the harbour, now the sky was dark with cloud, *Iskra* was streamed out on her buoy ropes, steady and secure, the wind still from the south but increasing, the shore a faint line to starboard, the trawler no more than a dark shape, close but insubstantial. I had a last look round. Everything was shipshape.

There was a sensual cosiness in the cabin as if the soft radiance of the oil lights, the warmth and the familiar luxury had blurred and smoothed the hard edges of life. We sat over our supper, a concoction of leftovers from which Wendy can always contrive a meal, toyed with the dregs of French wine.

"It hasn't been our best voyage," Wendy said, "it's been one thing after another, in a sort of cumulative pyramid – it makes me wonder what's going to happen next."

"Don't worry – we're nearly there – one more day's sail and she'll be hauled out and tucked under her cover and you and I will be on our way home for the winter."

Wendy said, "I'll be pleased to get home – this voyage has gone on for too long. Too much bad weather, too many headwinds, too many alarms. I want my nice home – the garden . . ."

"Well, we didn't have a headwind today," I said defensively. We washed up and went to bed, tucking ourselves into our sleeping bags. I could feel the uneven cadence of the wind, rising and falling as it streamed through *Iskra*'s ropes and wires, see the faint glow of the night through her round portholes, feel her pulling and worrying at her mooring. I went sound to sleep.

RESCUE AND RECOVERY

5

Shipwreck

Something woke me before daylight. I got up and looked at the cabin clock – 4.30. Wendy was awake. The wind was much stronger now, I could hear it, I could feel *Iskra* straining at the buoy like a nervous horse.

Wendy said, "It's blowing much harder – is she all right?"

"I'll go and look." I put on a sweater over my pyjamas, climbed into the cockpit, stood for a minute. This was a real gale – it had backed a point to south. As *Iskra* swung to the buoy the wind would catch her first on one side, then on the other, heeling her gently. I went for'ard with a torch, holding to the cabin rail and the lifeline, crawled across the foredeck to the stem, head bent against the wind. The ropes were fine. They were both bar-tight but neither of them was under too much strain. I put my hand on them, feeling their tension. I slacked each one a fraction to bring a new part of the rope to bear on the ring through the buoy. "Pity I didn't put the anchor chain on the buoy," I muttered. "Too late now. I'd never get in there." I went back into the cabin – Wendy had got dressed. "She's fine – don't worry – both ropes in good shape. We've lain to buoys before in as much wind as this."

I boiled the kettle, made a cup of cocoa, lit one of the oil lamps, got back into my bag still with my sweater on. "It's pretty cold and a bit wild on the foredeck but she's quite safe. Either of the ropes is strong enough to stand twice the strain." I knew Wendy wasn't convinced. She had apprehension, unease, written all over her face. I knew inside myself that when she is on edge, nervous, she usually has good cause. Sometimes she's right, sometimes she's wrong – I hope she's wrong this time, I thought to myself.

"You mustn't worry – she'll be all right."

"What would happen if the ropes broke?"

"We'd start the engine, drop the anchor." We sat with the hot mugs in our hands, the steamy aroma of cocoa enhancing the sense of steady assurance given off by *Iskra*'s cabin – the books, the brass lamps, mementoes of past voyages, the chart table, the brass fog-horn on the bulkhead inside the companion hatch. This was home, the warm cocoon we wrap around ourselves – this was warmth, safety. Then the wind dropped – in a moment it was calm.

I slid the hatch and looked out. It was black, calm, the night full of threat but the wind gone. Big drops of rain plopped straight down on the hatch, the cabin top, the furled sail, the sea beside me. Shafts of light from the cabin portholes probed the damp night, the raindrops filtering through them. I slammed the hatch shut. "There, the wind's gone. Perhaps that's the end of it – or the beginning of the end." I tapped the glass. It jumped down three millibars. It was strangely quiet in the cabin, the muted roar of the gale suddenly stilled, *Iskra* quiet, only the faint drumming of the rain. "When the wind comes before the rain, soon you may make sail again," I quoted more in hope than in conviction. "We'll go back to bed for an hour or so – it'll be light soon." I peeled off my sweater. The first flush of dawn was already paling the sky.

The wind came back with abrupt power, rain driven horizontally, a sudden cold tang in it. It seemed to hit *Iskra* like some solid object. She heeled slightly to starboard and then recovered herself. In minutes it was blowing harder than before, whining through the rigging again, its roar pitched higher, its force more potent – it was no longer passing overhead but blowing low down, no longer deflected by the shore. She began to pitch into it. Suddenly it was rough in Ardminish Bay. I looked at the compass. *Iskra* had swung towards the east, now she was pointing out into the open sound. In minutes she was rearing up and pitching into short, steep waves. We could feel her jerking herself against the buoy ropes.

We both heard it – a crack like a rifle shot. "Oh my God," I said and leapt for the hatch. Ardminish Bay was altogether changed. No longer protected by the point, there were waves with white crests in the Bay – I saw them in the advancing daylight as I crawled for'ard. One of the ropes was broken, the stranded end hanging down over my Dolphin's face. The remaining rope was jerking against the buoy ring as she rose and pitched. Wendy was already in the cockpit. I shouted to her "start the engine." As I gained the cockpit there was another report like the first, a shake, a shudder running through the boat. We were adrift.

The engine was running. I advanced the throttle, slammed it into gear, put the tiller hard over to starboard. Her bow was paying off the wind – to starboard towards the trawler. In seconds we were on top of her. The bowsprit caught the trawler's bow, dragged itself along her rail and entangled itself round an iron stanchion. *Iskra* swung alongside with a crash of splintering wood. She lay with her starboard side lifting on the waves and smashing against iron bulwarks. She shuddered at every impact, at every impact there was a gouging and rending of broken timber. "She'll tear herself adrift sooner or later – I'll try and get a line on." I pulled up the cockpit floor, grabbed a good mooring rope from the locker.

Iskra was shuddering and grinding at every impact. I crawled for'ard, holding to the handrail on the coach roof to stop myself from being hurled overboard. Each time she rose on a wave she hit the rusty sides of the trawler with all her weight behind each blow, like a boxer at a punchball – a hopeless fight with the odds stacked against her. The sound of the crushed and breaking timber cut into me like a knife. I glanced over my shoulder. Now it was light. I could see the rocks in jagged lines on either side of a concrete ramp – I guessed they were a quarter of a mile off, perhaps closer. The surf was hitting them, sending columns of spray and spume high in the air. "We wouldn't last five minutes in that," I muttered. *Iskra* was held alongside by her bowsprit in an iron grip. There was no way to force in a fender to protect her.

Each time she rose and fell the deck jumped so that I couldn't keep my feet, spray was flying over the bow, sometimes green water. The trawler was all iron projections, digging into *Iskra*'s topsides, smashing her rail. The noise was heavy with destruction – this was a grim fight she couldn't win. I saw an iron stanchion, part of a fishing gantry. It was almost beyond my reach. I stretched out for it, one hand holding to the lifeline, she gave a violent lurch and I fell into the scuppers, inches from certain injury. Wendy was beside me as I got to my feet. "Here – put it on – now," she passed me a lifejacket. I struggled into it over my pyjamas. She held on to it by the back, bracing herself against the shakes and shudders while I leaned out, passed the rope round the stanchion, made it fast with a bowline.

I left the rope slack, we both crawled back to the cockpit. We looked around Ardminish Bay. The wind seemed ever to increase, black clouds raced over, the shore was bleak, deserted – a few houses, the ferry terminal, the lines of rocks like devils' teeth, spewing white water, hurling it skyward so that it hung in a hazy curtain of blown spume. Now we could hardly hear ourselves speak above the roar of the wind, the deathly sound of *Iskra* grinding herself to pieces. "I'll get the anchor over the bow – she won't stay here long." I crawled for'ard again, crouched by the anchor, undid the lashings, pulled a few fathoms of chain up from the locker. My arm crooked round the fore stay for support I got the anchor over the bow. I had turned to go back to the cockpit when the bowsprit broke off short with a sudden crack of sound and a lurch as *Iskra* came free of the trawler. She was held for a moment by the bowsprit shroud – for long enough for me to take up the slack of the rope and turn it round the bitts. Then the wire shroud was wrenched free of its chainplate and the heavy spar, 13 feet long and 6 inches in diameter, fell into the sea, held alongside by the bobstay and by the furled up jib. The jib came slack, unrolled itself a few turns and began to flog with studied violence, flaying with its heavy block back and forth across the foredeck inches from my head with a noise like a machine gun. The rope took the strain. I knew it would break because the stanchion it was fast to was made of angle iron – the sharp edge of it would cut the rope. It was only a matter of minutes. I dragged out another rope, managed to still the worst of the flapping by tying the jib to the mast. I slacked the line to the trawler slowly to the end. For a few minutes she lay quietly, the line stretched bar tight. "She won't stay here long – it'll break for certain."

We both looked at the empty shore, the rocks, the seas breaking, the low cloud, the utter desolation. I looked at Wendy. She was ice calm but her face was drawn, her voice a monotone, devoid of emotion. I knew she knew that *Iskra* was doomed. By the look of it, we would be lucky to get away with our lives. I was wet and cold, almost insensible with cold. Wendy brought me out a pair of trousers, a thick jersey – helped me put them on over the wet pyjamas. Then I saw a buoy, another mooring buoy not more than 15 ft from our stern.

I said, "I'll swim for it with a rope – I'll be all right in my life-jacket."

She said, "No – no – no. You mustn't."

I was beyond argument. I said, "All right – then you must send a Mayday. They might get someone down to the shore to help us. Send it now." She went below. I heard her calm voice. "Mayday, Mayday – yacht *Iskra* in Ardminish Bay, Isle of Gigha, two on board. We are in danger of running on rocks and need assistance." She sent it twice, there was no answer.

We sat for a moment in silence in the bottom of the cockpit, the gale screaming over us. The engine was still running ahead. I could hardly think – I was too cold. Perhaps I could reef her and sail her out of the Bay with three tucks in the main and the stays'l. She would never sail with the bowsprit in the water alongside. It would take too long there wasn't time. We looked at the surf and shuddered, searched the bleak shore for a sign of life. Perhaps the anchor would hold – I doubted it. The bottom, I guessed, was covered in kelp, the anchor would drag over it. Then a fierce squall of wind and rain, laid on top of the gale, broke the rope with a dull thud and she was adrift again. Her bow turned away from the wind and she was off – helter-skelter for the rocks to lee'ard.

Wendy put the engine in neutral, I dragged myself for'ard again, my hands hardly obeying my fuddled brain, got the turns of chain off the bitts. The anchor plunged down, dragging the chain across the deck with enormous force. I couldn't stop it. "Christ, it'll break the lashing in the chain locker and go overboard." I seized the loose jib, laid it over the chain and stood on it. It held up for an instant – long enough for me to take turns round the bitts. The chain came bar tight with a jerk – *Iskra* swung into the wind. It was holding. Now she was close to the ferry ramp, just clear of the surf.

We watched her. Wendy said, "There's a house on the shore, on the other side of the bay, in line with the end of the ramp – you watch her, I'll go in and get a bag ready."

At first she was steady and then the bearings began to slip apart.

"She's dragging," I shouted "you'd better come up." Now the rocks were close aboard.

"Shall we swim for it?"

"No – its better to stay with her." I gripped Wendy's hand. We waited for the first crash of rock on her bottom. Now the fine spray was all over us, the noise of the surf all around us.

Suddenly there was another crushing blast of noise and the helicopter was over us. The Mayday – I'd forgotten about it. The machine hovered above our stern, quite close. Two men in the open hatch were gesticulating, waving their arms and pointing at *Iskra*'s mast – trying to tell us something. Wendy was shouting at me, her lips moving but no sound over the roar of the machine. There was nothing except this overwhelming noise that drowned all thought, all sense. Slowly I realised what it was. Something inside me clicked like a switch and I was able to move. Slowly some strength came back to me through the cold – my brain ground itself laboriously into action. The topping lift – the runners – everything abaft the mast must be moved out of the way – of course. I unclipped the runners, tied them with their lashings to the shrouds, cut the topping lift, overhauled the peak halyard through the blocks, leaving the long rope in an untidy heap on the deck.

Wendy came up with a small kit bag – money, ship's papers, a few essentials. A man in a wet suit came swinging down out of the sky. At first the rope dumped him into the sea astern, then he was plucked out of it and hovered for a moment a foot off *Iskra*'s stern, the wind swinging him away and then close to the boat. Wendy grabbed his hand, pulled him in until he gained foothold on the narrow after deck by the boom gallows. He grabbed her, turned her round and slipped a padded belt over her head and under her arms. He took the kit bag out of her hand, shook his head and dropped it into the cockpit. Then she was gone, clasped in his arms, his legs tightly gripping her body, sailing aloft – to Heaven perhaps. The thought came to me "She'll never come back." I was alone, abandoned, sad, broken. Once before in my life I had lost a beautiful yacht – now another. Everything I loved was going. I was in a state of shock – my capacity to think and act had left me. I was cold – teeth chattering. It didn't occur to me that the man would come back for me. I stood like an idiot, gazing blankly upwards.

He did come back, swinging down as before. I felt his firm hands round my waist too, felt myself swept away, suddenly weightless and free, gyrating slowly round, the world turning round me. I saw the Sound of Gigha, the coast of Kintyre across it, the white horses in the sea, the island laid out like a model in a museum. *Iskra*'s mast came swinging round just under my feet, her burgee flat and stiff in the wind, the rocks within feet of her, the surf already reaching out to clasp her in a rocky embrace, behind her the ferry ramp. Now there was a car drawn up, two men beside it, their heads turned upwards. Then I was being dragged into the helicopter, strong hands pulling me over the smooth, aluminium cill.

Wendy was there, sitting on a low seat, I slumped beside her. She put her arms round me and hugged.

As the machine circled round I saw *Iskra* again, hard against the shore. I saw smoke from her exhaust. "Oh Christ," I said, "I left the bloody engine running." One of the crew was standing beside me. I pulled at his leg and he bent down and put his ear beside my mouth. It was quieter inside the machine. "Don't take us away," I shouted, "land us here." He spoke to the pilot, came back, nodded his head. The machine circled round, landed on a square of concrete in the lee of the shed. I was helped out, managed to shake hands with the crew, mumbled words of thanks. Wendy gave them each a big kiss. The blank look had left her, her voice came with its old ring, the flatness gone. With a last roar they were away, we watched them sail gracefully back across the Sound. We were bundled into the car. As it turned I saw *Iskra* hit the rocks.

6

Despair

We were taken to the Coastguard store – a low room full of buoys and nets and gear, up a flight of wooden steps over the old boathouse, now a café. I was given dry trousers, dry socks and a voluminous sweater. I was too cold to be able to put them on, my teeth had stopped chattering. Wendy sat me on the floor and between them they pulled off my wet clothes, forced the dry clothes on. Then we were shepherded out and into the car again, driven for a mile and ushered into John Martin's house. He was the chief volunteer coastguard of Gigha. In minutes there was a roaring fire, cups of tea and John was running a hot bath. We sat in it together, feet towards the middle, felt the warmth spreading through our bodies. My teeth started to chatter again and then they stopped as the circulation came back. It took half an hour for me to get warm. Then there was an enormous breakfast, more cups of steaming tea, another log on the fire. Slowly, through the euphoria induced by warmth and food and hot tea and the blazing fire the enormity of what had happened flooded into my mind. I said to John, "I must go back to the boat – I must go and have a look at her." At that moment the Minister arrived in a car with his daughter Miriam. "We'll take you," he said, "you can see her right in front of you from our house."

We went back along the straight road, through the village and down a short road towards the sea. The Manse overlooks Ardminish Bay, the view stretches across to the Kintyre shore. Now the Sound was calmer, the wind had taken off. We could see the buoy we had been tied to, the trawler, securely chained to the next one, the ferry ramp. *Iskra* was perched up on a line of rocks, close below the house, the water still round her

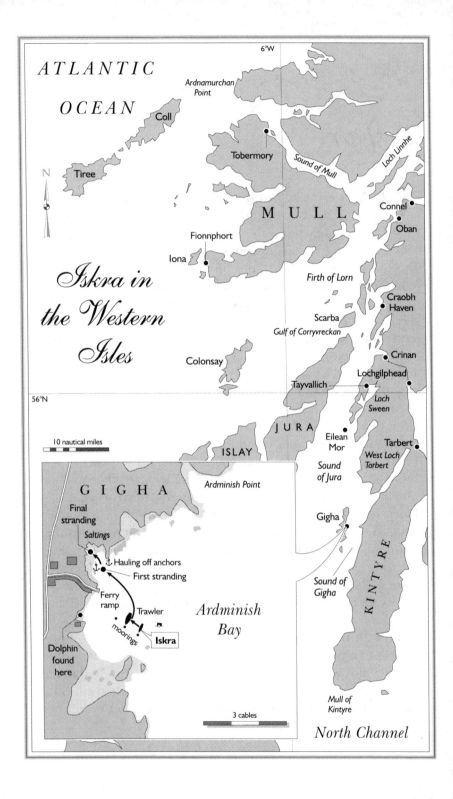

ATLANTIC

OCEAN

Coll

Tiree

N

*Iskra in
the Western
Isles*

56°N

10 nautical miles

6°W

Ardnamurchan
Point

Tobermory

Sound of Mull

Loch Linnhe

MULL

Connel

Oban

Fionnphort

Iona

Firth of Lorn

Craobh
Haven

Scarba

Gulf of Corryvreckan

Crinan

Lochgilphead

Colonsay

Tayvallich

Loch
Sween

JURA

Eilean
Mor

Tarbert

West Loch
Tarbert

ISLAY

Ardminish Point

Sound
of Jura

Gigha

GIGHA

Final
stranding

Saltings

⚓ Hauling off anchors

First stranding

Ferry
ramp

Trawler

moorings

Iskra

*Ardminish
Bay*

Sound of
Gigha

KINTYRE

Dolphin
found
here

3 cables

Mull of
Kintyre

North Channel

keel. Incredibly, the engine was still running – I could see the exhaust smoke.

"I must go down there at once," I said, "I may be able to get on board."

The Minister was scathing. "You must have rotten gear," he said, "why couldn't you anchor again, or tie to another buoy?"

Miriam took us to the ferry ramp in the car. *Iskra* was a few yards to the north of the ramp. She was on a line of rocks some 20 yards off-shore, across a rock pool. A few people in a group were looking at her. I wanted to swim out across the pool – Wendy wouldn't hear of it. "See if you can borrow a boat," she said. There was a short, stocky man with greying hair, clear, far-seeing eyes, a seaman for certain. He had the gait and bearing of a seaman. "Aye," he said, "there's a wee small plastic boat you can be borrowing." We walked across to a rill on the other side of the ramp. Graham thought we would be able to get her off on the high tide the next day. She was clinging to the edge of a rock shelf, he said, her keel must be very close to deep water. A strong pull from the top of her mast would shift her off. "Aye – I'll be putting a good anchor out tomorrow morning, when it calms down." Graham's motor cruiser was berthed in the rill, tied securely from both quarters and lying to a stout chain mooring. We carried the little dinghy back, I launched it into the pool. The wind was lighter now but surf was still breaking against the rocks and there was swell, even in the pool. *Iskra* was lying with a slight list to starboard. I grabbed her starboard shroud and hauled myself aboard, making the dinghy fast to the shrouds, abaft the shattered topsides and deck. I slid open the hatch. A cloud of exhaust smoke billowed out – the cabin was full of exhaust. I climbed into the cockpit, reached down for the throttle and pulled it up. The engine slowly ticked to a stop. Incredible. The engine is pushing 50 years old – it must have been running for hours without circulating water.

When the fumes cleared I went below. It was chaos, she was half full of oily water. She must be holed somewhere under her starboard bilge, hard against the rocks now. The engine was almost red hot, the exhaust had broken in half. *Iskra* was unsteady. She shook whenever a heavy surf reached her keel or a strong gust of wind hit her. I looked around in shocked despair. Wendy's locker on the port side had sprung open spewing its contents into the oily bilge, now nearly a foot deep over the cabin sole. Some of her belongings were floating among the scum in a forlorn jumble. I rescued a hair brush and her handbag. Half the contents of a bookshelf had been wrenched free and were half submerged, the chart was spread out over the mess as if to hide it from view, one of the lamp glasses had been smashed. She must have hit the rock with a cruel crash. It was as if some wanton vandal had been at work. The water had been higher – up to the side cushions – they were soaked and filthy. She must be badly stove in. I felt a melancholy despair seep into me. I was incapable of action – I could see nothing profitable to do.

In the half-hour I had been on board the wind had increased again, quickly kicking up a short chop across the pond between *Iskra* and the shore. I looked at it and went below again, waded through the muck to the locker amidships and found a life-jacket. I retrieved the kit bag from the cockpit floor, put it in Graham's dinghy with what I had collected together, gingerly got on board and undid the painter. Before I could ship the oars a surf picked up the dinghy and swept it on to the rocks close by *Iskra*'s stern. Another sea picked it up again and smashed it down, splintering its frail hull. I had to leave it, hauled out on the rocks and tied to *Iskra*'s stern, the oars under the thwart. From the rock I was able to look along *Iskra*'s port side – as far as I could see it wasn't damaged, there wasn't a mark on it. I half-waded, half-swam to the shore, the kit bag held above my head out of the water, and scrambled up the rocks. I was cold again – not as cold as before. Wendy and Miriam bundled me into the car, took me back to the Minister's house. I stood dripping in his porch, was given more trousers, another sweater, a voluminous track suit. The Minister was a very large man.

First Stranding.

Second Stranding.

Deep into the cove – at high water.

We walked disconsolately back to John's house. It had started to rain, a fine wetting Scotch rain, we were both wet by the time we gained his warm kitchen. John lived alone, his wife had died, his children were away from the island. He was at work but he had told us to make ourselves at home.

"Be treating the place as if it were your own." We had some lunch, tried to think what to do.

"As soon as it calms down I'll get aboard again and bring our rubber dinghy off," I said. "At least we'll be able to get some clothes ashore. I'll have to write to the insurance company and tell them what's happened." John's kitchen was already hung with my own and the Minister's and the coastguards' clothes.

Graham, we discovered, lived on the opposite side of the road. We knocked at his door, were at once asked in to his snug living room. Graham had been at sea during the War, we had a lot in common. He had been skipper of the ferry that runs between Gigha and Tayinloan on the other side of the Sound. Now he was retired, owned the fine cabin cruiser we had seen in the rill. There was little he didn't know about the weather, the tides, the shoreline of Gigha.

I said, "I'm sorry about the little boat Graham – of course I'll pay for the repair."

"Och no – its nothing. I'll be repairing it in the winter, I'm thinking – give me a wee job to do."

Graham took us back to the ferry ramp in his car. The wind had eased. We went back to *Iskra* in Graham's pulling boat, a punt he called it, collected his plastic dinghy off the rock. We brought ashore our own rubber dinghy from under the cockpit floor and put it in the ferry waiting room. While I was on board, I pumped as much water as I could with the hand pump – it had been up to within an inch of the top of the batteries.

While Wendy cooked us a meal I telephoned Adrian at home in Maldon on John's phone. It rang for minutes before he answered – I had just caught him. "I've wrecked *Iskra* on the rocks in Gigha. She's badly holed. We might get her off tomorrow but even if we do, I'm not sure whether we will be able to keep her afloat until we can beach her."

"Are you and Wendy all right?"

"Yes – we were taken off by a helicopter."

He said, "I'll 'phone you back this evening at half past seven. I was just going off for a few days. I heard the 'phone as I was closing the door behind me."

I sat down in front of John's fire and wrote a letter to Guardian Insurance. I would just have time before John came home from work. I had been paying my premiums for years, had never made a claim, had never had any other contact with the insurance company. I told them, briefly, what had happened, ended with the words, 'my concern is that the vessel should be re-floated and taken to a safe haven as soon as possible.'

As I wrote down the sad story my own complicity in *Iskra*'s distress was brought home to me. Perhaps the Minister's scorn was justified. I could have put the anchor chain on the buoy as soon as we arrived – the gale was well forecast, I could have seen that the buoy was open to the south-east. I could have thrown the anchor over the bulwarks of the trawler and slacked chain as soon as she came adrift, allowing her to lie safely until the gale abated. I ought to have a proper rope ready for tying to a buoy, with an iron thimble spliced into the end and a big shackle for the buoy ring. We would have had a damaged boat, but we would have had a boat – now I doubted whether *Iskra* would survive. I ought to have got dressed, as Wendy had done, as soon as danger showed itself – then I would have been warm and dry and able to use my head, to think instead of grasping at one expedient after another. I know quite well that a cold man, like a tired man, is a danger to himself and his boat. I ought to have learned the lessons I have so often preached.

I would not have sent the Mayday if I had been thinking properly. A Pan Pan, asking for assistance from the shore, would have sufficed to alert the coastguards. As it was, the Mayday was picked up by an Oyster 68 sail training ketch, the

Lord Rank, on passage between Belfast and Islay. Mark Oliver, her skipper, was listening on Channel 16. He picked up a weak signal and a minute later another. He was about 20 miles to the south. He replied to it but heard nothing more, he then relayed it to the Clyde Coastguard. Two Royal Navy ships were in the area but too far off to lend assistance. The Coastguard asked Mark whether he could help, but he replied that his ship was running before a Force 10 wind, with ropes streamed astern. She was rolling heavily in big seas, he had children on board. There was nothing he could do to help. The helicopter, we were told, was sent from Culross, on the Firth of Forth. The crew were a model – calm, competent and at the same time concerned and sympathetic.

Adrian telephoned as promised, "I'm coming up on a 'plane tomorrow – I'll have to spend a night somewhere but I'll be with you on Tuesday – there's a ferry at mid-day."

I said, "I hope you're not wasting your time. I think she'll sink as soon as she comes off the rock."

He asked me a lot of questions about Gigha. Was there a yard anywhere near? No. Was the beach close to where she was? No. Could we stop the leak from inside? No. Was there anyone around who could help us? Yes. At least one, probably more.

"If she sinks we'll get flotation bags and raise her."

As I put the 'phone down John arrived home. We had supper in silence. It was blowing again – we could hear the wind in the chimney and through the trees outside – another gale, from the south-west this time. "*Iskra*'s in the lee of the island this time," I thought. We were exhausted after a day that had seemed to go on forever, from one disaster to another. Even Adrian's enthusiasm and his promise of help had not raised my spirits. We tumbled into John's beds at half past nine, went straight to sleep.

Within an hour John came in and roused us, shaking us to wake us from a deep sleep. "The Minister's here. He says *Iskra*'s afloat." We got up, and put on our clothes.

"Hurry up," the Minister said, "your boat's off the rocks

and afloat – all you have to do is go aboard, pick up the anchor and tie her to the buoy." I knew he was wrong but we went with him meekly. I was too demoralised to offer resistance. It was high tide, she had come off the rock as he said, the change of wind had blown her off the ledge. She appeared to be lying to her anchor a few yards off-shore. We could see her dimly – not clear enough to tell whether she was aground or afloat. Wendy said, "Don't go – it's dangerous." The surf was breaking on the rocks but not as fiercely as before. It looked menacing. Seeing me hesitate, the Minister said, "Go on – if you don't get her now you'll never get her." I knew it was useless but I was in no state to stand up to this onslaught. His voice had an edge of scorn in it. I dragged the rubber dinghy out from the ferry terminal, pumped it up in the lee of a shed, dragged it to the water a few yards from the concrete ramp.

As I rowed out through the surf the Minister switched on the lights of his car, lighting an eerie spectacle. *Iskra* was surrounded by rocks, hard aground and bumping as the swell came in, the short seas hitting her smashed topsides, washing over her deck, the broken bowsprit crashing against her. It was a scene of hopeless dejection. I managed to get the dinghy alongside, climbed aboard with some difficulty. She was already half full of water. It was hopeless – there was nothing I could do. The engine had no exhaust, although I could probably run it. The anchor chain was slack. I pulled it in a few feet and then it caught – behind a rock probably. I pulled as hard as I could but it was useless. If anything she was going back towards another maze of rocks. I came ashore, wetting my clothes for the third time, left the dinghy tied to a rock on the shore. "Hopeless," I said. The Minister drove us home.

The next day was fine – a light westerly breeze, bright sunshine. We walked through the village, stopped at the shop and post office, bought some groceries, posted my letter to the insurance company. Mrs. McSporran was a small, round, busy lady with quick eyes, and a kind face. She was the post mistress. Clearly she and her husband Seamus were in charge of the whole island. The shop had everything from mouse traps to Wellington boots, there were half a dozen customers, all conversation came to a stop when we came in. I told Mrs. McSporran we were from the yacht aground in the bay. "Oh aye," she said, "that's right enough."

We walked on down to the ferry ramp, the road commanding a panorama of the Sound, the whole of Ardminish Bay, a jetty to the right where the Coastguard store was, the buoy we had tied to and the rocks behind, the ferry ramp and the Manse close up the hill. The island had the feel of freedom and space, the bays and rocky points and bright sands and green swards, all sparkling clean in the morning sunshine spoke of the joy to be found in a beautiful place, the joy of islands. At first *Iskra* was nowhere to be seen and then, as we opened out the narrow bay beside the ferry we saw her leaning mast. She had been swept almost to the end of a shallow cove. It was just past high water, she was lying over on her port side on a patch of fine, clean sand, her bow towards us, surrounded by rocks. We sat on a tuft of grass and looked at her in disbelief. There were a few inches of water round her keel. In Gigha, there is no more than a four foot rise and fall of the tide – *Iskra* draws 5 feet 6 inches. We looked at each other and then at *Iskra* again. We both saw it at the same time.

"The Dolphin – he's gone, jumped ship – disappeared."

I said, "We've lost her, we'll never get her out of here – no possible chance. She's there to stay. I'm going to tell Adrian not to come."

A big, crystal tear rolled down Wendy's cheek.

7

Hope Rekindled

To lose a ship is to lose a part of yourself that cannot easily be replaced. The wrecking of *Girl Stella* in Flores had a profound effect on my whole life. Even after a lapse of 25 years I still look back on that terrible night in Porto Piqueran with horror – it was a nightmare that never went away. Like *Iskra*, only perhaps more so, the *Girl Stella* was a thing of beauty. Her value could only be counted in terms outside the narrow limits of pounds, shillings and pence. She was irreplaceable. She was a gaff ketch of 24 tons, built as a West Country lugger in 1895. She had been converted to a yacht in 1935 by a man with impeccable taste and flair, a man with an instinct for what is excellent and the means to achieve it. She was a delight to be aboard – full of grace and comfort, at the same time an easy and pleasant home. On deck she was a real ship – massively built of teak and oak and pitch pine, well masted, well rigged, her gear carefully thought out. She was heavy but she could be handled comfortably by two men or a man and a boy. She was an enchantress to sail – in light airs she would glide to windward with her tall sails, in a hard blow she showed her power and weight, her ability to thunder through heavy seas. I found her in Will and Alf Drakes' yard in Tollesbury, she had been neglected for years. She was run down, poorly thought of, poorly loved; it took years to bring her back to her glory. When she was wrecked I was devastated.

If you are the captain of a ship, a big ship or a little ship, there is no escaping responsibility for her. It is one of the immutable laws of the sea. There may be extenuating circumstances, unforeseen or unaccountable happenings but ultimately, the captain has to take the blame. It is he who must gauge every risk, see every danger, anticipate every possible pitfall for his ship and take the right action in good time. If the ship is lost he may be exonerated but he always knows, if he looks into his own soul, that if he had acted differently she would have been saved. I know that I was responsible for *Girl Stella*'s loss although no person sought to blame me. I knew now, as we sat on that tuft of grass, that I carried the same weight for *Iskra*.

Wendy said, "We ought to get the gear off her." We went on board, gazed around at the wreckage. In place of the homely warmth and comfort we had left a few hours earlier there was a heap of filthy wreckage. She was lying over on her port side now – the side that was undamaged. Black, oily water covered Wendy's bunk, was half way up her locker, the flotsam of our belongings strewn dejectedly across the cabin. The water had been up the starboard side too, had soaked my bunk and had left an oily tide mark. Once again it had not reached the top of the batteries by inches – the electrics were still working except the electric pump which I had left running with the engine. It was seized solid. I pumped her dry with the hand pump. We collected up loose gear, wiped it clean and passed it into the cockpit. It was cold, wet, depressing.

We worked in silence. Wendy saved tins of food from the lockers, the soaked and spoiled remains of her possessions, our sleeping bags, oozing filth, her clothes, most of them undamaged from the high shelves over the lavatory. We spoke little, it was hard to find anything of good cheer to say. I took out the instruments, my sextant, also stowed in the lavatory, was undamaged. The chronometer, still ticking bravely, the VHF radio, compass, direction finder were all passed out, ferried to the shore in the rubber dinghy. We made a mound of our gear in the ferry waiting room. We saw the ferry come and go half a dozen times in the day. We brought our bicycles ashore, they were safe, stowed on the high bunk in the fo'c'sle, used them to go home to John's house to have lunch. I 'phoned Adrian but there was no reply. "He must be on his way – nothing will stop him coming now." There was a foot of water round *Iskra* at low tide, little more than three feet at high tide, not enough to bring her on an even keel, let alone float her.

It was hopeless – I could see no way to get her off unless another south-east gale brought another exceptional tide and if that happened, she would only be driven further into the cove. I said to Wendy, "It would be nice to go home, forget the whole thing." The fight had gone out of me, something that had never happened to me before. I remember a strange feeling of relief. The sailing business was at an end, I was finished with it, the responsibility was suddenly lifted. I had the same feeling when the *Girl Stella* sank in Porto Piqueran – thank God, it's over. I had counted them as we all stood shivering on the stone quay, dripping from the sea – Adrian, Patrick, Celia, Dick, all safe thank God.

As soon as we could get out of this place we would go home, start doing something else, find some other occupation – gardening perhaps. It had been a long innings. I had taken chances, got away with it over and over again. This time I had played with the sea once too often, it had turned round and bitten me. The sea wields a monumental justice, does not suffer gladly those who treat it lightly, those who offend against its unchanging laws. Perhaps it was right, within the order of things, that I should be brought up with a round turn. At least no one had lost a life through my failures and misfortunes over the years. I would stop now, before I took a step too far. It was a sudden relief to be free of the whole thing, to be able to put it all behind me.

A boat is like a child that never grows up. I had been fussing and worrying about *Iskra* for twenty-five years, I had spent all my leisure time looking after her and her predecessors for as long as I could remember. I had neglected every other aspect of life, like a man with tunnel vision. There were great avenues of experience open to me I had never had the time to explore. Now I was released, set free to wander the wide realms of new experience, new understanding.

We worked until evening, had our supper with John. I offered to move into the hotel in the village but he wouldn't hear of it. "You'll be staying for as long as it takes to get her off." Graham, too, was optimistic. "In a couple of days we'll see another big tide," he said. I was unconvinced. We went to bed and slept long and deep. Sleep dispelled much of the gloom – it didn't take away the pessimism.

"I still don't see how she's ever going to come out of there," I said to Wendy as we rode our bikes back to *Iskra.* "We'll try and save as much gear as we can."

"Perhaps Adrian will have some new ideas," she replied, "he'll be here this morning."

I had half forgotten he was coming. I ought to get a patch over that leak – if the tide did come up in the evening, she would fill with water again. The thought of Adrian arriving jolted the self pity out of me. We stopped at Mrs. McSporran's on our way past, did some shopping for John, ordered coal for his fire. Vie Tulloch was in the shop. "If you want anything moved to John's house," she said "I'll take it in my car for you. Let me know if I can help you . . ." We thanked her, said we would take her up on the offer.

Iskra hadn't moved in the night. There was still a foot of water round her, the tide hadn't even come up to her leak, she had no water in her. I climbed aboard, made my way to the fo'c'sle, groped under all the gear and found my sheet of lead. Copper nails, a hammer, a pair of snips were all to hand. I found a tube of sealing compound, caulking cotton, a chisel I use for a caulking iron. We stood in the dinghy, Wendy holding the boat steady alongside. The copper sheathing was all torn away, hanging in sheets where it had been wrenched away from the hull. We cut it back with the snips so that we could get at the damage. I offered the patch to the broken plank. It covered the hole with two inches to spare at either end. We spread the sealer over the back of the patch, slapped it on and secured it with a nail. While Wendy held the dinghy steady I hammered in nails and tacks all round the patch. I filled three split seams with cotton, hammered it in with the iron and covered the whole job with sealer. The broken bowsprit was still lying alongside in the water. We cleared away the bowsprit shrouds, unshackled the forestay and carried the broken spar into the shed.

She had come through a dog-leg of rocks to find the only patch of clean sand in the cove; it was hard to see how she had done it. She lay with her bow tucked behind a rounded rock about three feet high. She must have swivelled round on her stern post to position herself so exactly – the sharp end of her keel had dug itself into the sand. It was a chance in a thousand – the only level, clear space in this rock strewn cove. By another chance she had fallen on her port side with her starboard side facing upwards. We would not have been able to find and stop the leak if she had fallen the other way. As we dragged the bowsprit ashore a sudden shaft of sunlight caught her in its beam. We stood side by side and looked at her, Wendy slid her hand into mine.

It was hard to believe that this friend who had been with us for so long, had stood by us and been our strength over the years, had come to her last resting place. It was as hard to see how she could ever retrace her path, hard again to see how we were to conduct our lives without her. In her broken state she had kept her dignity, the subtle aura of security and stability she gave out was still to be felt. Her bowsprit was a jagged stump, her tiller was smashed, her rudder torn off, hanging by one pintle, her very keel wrenched to one side, her starboard topsides and rail stove in – a hundred other more or less serious ills no doubt. My Dolphin had gone, back to the sea where his free spirit always lived. He must have taken my spirit with him. Yet she didn't give out the message of doom that a wreck gives out, you couldn't look at her and say "she's finished."

Wendy said, "Surely she can be got out somehow – I can't believe she's going to end her days here."

I said, "You would think so but I can't see how it is going to happen." Then the ferry arrived, bringing Adrian.

Adrian is a professional seaman of wide experience and undoubted competence. He has sailed as skipper or as crew in every type of yacht – the big schooners of the West Indies, ocean racers, cruising yachts, smacks and Thames barges, his special love. He does not easily let things stand in his way when he embarks on a project. Adrian's commitment to *Iskra* is as deep as mine – as a boy he was with me when we sailed her home to Maldon from the River Orwell the day I bought her. As a small boy he was with me when *Girl Stella* was wrecked. He showed steady nerves on that occasion, he has had them ever since. As a yacht deliverer he has made countless voyages over the Atlantic Ocean and to the Pacific, in all manner of boats and with all manner of crews.

Adrian had made two friends on the trip across the Sound – they all came bounding over the saltings. He waved a greeting and looked round briefly, taking in every detail. His new friends were both divers, they had their equipment with them and in minutes they were in the water with their wet suits and snorkels. Between them they surveyed the entrance to the cove, shouting back directions and marks to Adrian, working out the route *Iskra* must follow to gain deep water. In half an hour they had given him a clear picture of the cove which lodged itself in his brain. Between us all we lifted the heavy rudder, cutting it free of its one remaining pintle, the divers carried it to the bank and laid it on the shore. Then we took off the steering vane. They looked at the under-side of the hull, on the port side. There was no damage that they could see. They went off with a cheery wave and wishes of good luck. "We'll need all the gear off," Adrian said, "the inside ballast out, every moveable thing taken ashore." And then he added, a stern note in his voice, "if this boat is to come off we must be absolutely single minded about it."

Graham came down to the shore and met Adrian – they got on together at once, each one instinctively grasping the other's meaning. Graham said he would lend his punt to get the ballast off, lay out a heavy anchor for us. We walked over to the boathouse for a quick lunch. The café was run by Vie's daughter Catriona – Vie was there.

"We need a really strong motor boat to tow her," Adrian said, "and some really strong, long rope."

Vie said, "Go and see Archie when he comes home from the fishing this evening. The *Marie D'Or's* got all the power in the world. Iain Wilkieson would help – he's a very useful man, you could ask Roddy to help, he's another diver."

I telephoned him at once, he agreed to come in the morning. Vie told us about a Russian fish factory ship that had been severely damaged in a storm in the Irish Sea in December. The crew were lifted off by helicopter, the captain had been injured and was taken to hospital in Ayrshire. The ship drove ashore on the rocks of north-west Gigha. "A lot of things were stolen from the wreck," she said, "rope and wire and nets and all manner of gear found its way ashore – the crew's clothing and all their personal possessions were stolen. We were very upset about it on Gigha because we felt the island had been let down. A lot of us clubbed together, raised a fair sum of money and sent it to the captain for himself and the crew." Then she gave me a small piece of advice that stood us in good stead. "If you want help in this island," she said, "you must ask for it. No one will offer but if you ask they'll give you everything they have."

We worked all afternoon, carried the heavy mains'l ashore, floated the boom and the gaff to the shore, stripped the halyards and all running rigging off the mast. Adrian climbed aloft, took off the double block for the throat halyard. "We'll need all the rope and blocks we can get and it will help to lighten her." The anchor and all the chain came off, the lockers were stripped out of every moveable thing, the ferry waiting room was converted into a store for *Iskra's* gear. People we met on the shore came and helped us carry our belongings across to the waiting room. We made a neat stow so that everything could be found when the time came. Adrian had taken charge of the operation, had infused it with his determination and optimism. I did what I was told – willingly, without rancour, only relief that someone had moved in.

"You'll have to bring back the VHF," he said, "we'll need it." We worked until evening, exchanging few words. I asked Mrs.

McSporran where I could find Archie McAllister. "Just across the road," she said, "next to the school. You should find him at home now."

I knocked at his door. His wife Lorna was the school teacher. "He'll be home just now." The *Marie D'Or* lay alongside the old pier in a bay two miles to the south – she was dredging for scallops in the Sound every day. Archie knew the whole story – the whole island knew it. "Aye," he said, "I'll do what I can – you can call me on channel 8; we'll come in from the fishing if need be. Ye'll be needing to turn her towards the sea and bring her out a wee bit." I told him it might be tomorrow, might be the next day. After that the tides would start to take off.

The mood had changed from the negative to the positive but I was still dubious. "She's heavy – we'll never move her unless the tide comes up more than four feet – and she's behind a large rock. Even without the ballast, she weighs more than 10 tons." No one was impressed. Adrian would not hear of defeat. "If she won't come on the next tide, we'll get flotation bags – she'll come. She's got to." He had worked out a plan.

We were all exhausted. John found another bed for Adrian. His house was hung about with our belongings, our washing was drying all across his kitchen, every corner was stuffed with our clothing, newly washed or waiting to be washed. His washing machine was broken down, waiting for the repair man to come from the mainland. Wendy spent every spare minute she could find kneeling over John's bath scrubbing, rinsing and wringing out washing. We took the Minister's clothes back to him, returned to their owners the miscellaneous garments I had borrowed. John is a joiner by trade. He put up with us, indeed wouldn't hear of our moving out, with remarkable goodwill and boundless hospitality. I got up and made tea early in the morning and the three of us went down to *Iskra*. "We've got a lot to do today," Adrian said.

We began to rig tackles. She would have to be hauled over the rock under her forefoot, she couldn't be pulled astern because the end of the keel had dug itself into the sand. *Iskra* carries two spare anchors on board, both large fisherman anchors. We secured one behind a big rock some 20 yards over on her port side and to this we led our strongest tackle. It was a purchase made up of *Iskra*'s throat halyard block and the double block from the main sheet. We joined together the strongest of the ropes we had and brought the tackle from the bitts for'ard to the rock, the hauling part leading right across the cove to the shore on the other side. This was to haul her over the rock and turn her. The other anchor was fixed behind another rock on the next part of the dog-leg. Graham came down with Iain Wilkieson and a long length of heavy rope, 3½ or 4 inches circumference. They laid a big fisherman anchor out through the middle of the cove to deep water where the *Marie D'Or* would be able to come in.

We started to unload ballast. A line of helpers appeared miraculously out of nowhere, the heavy, oily, dirty pigs of iron and lead were passed from hand to hand and stacked neatly on another rock at the side of the cove. We took another long length of rope, fastened it to *Iskra*'s stays'l halyard which hangs below the hounds and the cross trees, took the end to another rock across the cove. Soon, a ton of ballast was cleared out. Everything was stripped out of her, even the cabin floor boards. Only the VHF was still in place. Tired and dirty, we all trooped over to Catriona's café for a late lunch.

Everyone came back after lunch. There must have been upwards of 20 people round the cove. It was raining, the glass was tumbling, black clouds were building up, the tide had started to make, *Iskra* was beginning to lift. Roddy was there with yet another long, heavy rope. We fashioned a cradle round her hull, so that the strain of the tow would fall evenly round her, Roddy dived under and passed the end along the port side, we held the cradle in place with lines up to the deck, hauled it as tight as we could and made an eye in the end. The anchor rope was fastened to it. Now there were eight strong men on the bank. They lay on the tackle in a line across the shore.

They heaved, slow and steady – they were seamen, the sons of generations of seamen and they knew their business. Adrian was left on board *Iskra*. He took the fall of the stays'l halyard to *Iskra*'s mast winch and bowsed down, putting a heavy strain on the mast as he careened *Iskra* over on her side to lessen her draft. They heaved in unison. As the strain came on the tackle the block fast to the anchor suddenly turned itself round half a dozen turns, twisting the tackle, increasing friction and bringing the operation to a standstill. I went out in the rubber dinghy with a boat hook, passed it through the parts of the tackle and twisted it back until it was clear. I stayed in the dinghy holding the boat hook as they pulled.

The tackle came bar tight, rigid with strain. *Iskra* didn't budge. Graham had a handy billy ready. One end was fastened round a rock and the other to the hauling part of the tackle with a rolling hitch. They pulled again, now with an extra purchase, an advantage of 12 to 1. The rope broke with a dull, dead sound. They all tumbled to the ground, an untidy heap of flailing arms and up-ended sea boots. No one laughed. A splice in one of the ropes had given way. I knotted it together and pulling went on. She hadn't shifted. This time they gave all they had, the tackle was like high tension wire. I watched it stretch and strain, expecting it to break. I hung on to the boat hook to stop it turning – I saw it move, the parts sliding slowly, slowly through the block. She was coming.

She came inch by painful inch over the rock, her forefoot hard against it with all her weight inching itself up its smooth surface. If the rock had been jagged it wouldn't have been possible – another chance. This boat has a life wish, I thought. Wendy was on the shore, watching, dancing with excitement. Adrian hove down on the mast, *Iskra* careened over, our team of helpers dug their heels into the soft ground and lay back on the rope, Iain and Graham on the handy billy. *Iskra* moved round. As she came, she came more easily. It was nearly high tide. Soon she was clear of the rock, still heeling over 20 degrees.

Now the tackle was hove up two blocks and would move no

Adrian.

Bridle and bowline in position.

Free and away!

more. We overhauled it, Roddy dragging it to the second anchor. Another long, strong rope appeared from somewhere. They hove again, Adrian still bowsing down on the mast. She came another few feet round the dog-leg, enough for her to see open water ahead and on her starboard side. There were still two big rocks in her path. "She'll be coming on tomorrow's tide," Graham said. Our helpers shuffled off, coats turned up against the drizzle, home to tea well deserved. In moments the shore was deserted except for Adrian, Wendy and me.

It was the time of high water but the tide seemed still to be making. We recovered the tackles and piled them with an assortment of *Iskra*'s gear in a heap on the shore. The first gusts of wind came out of the south east – the wind that had put us on the rocks. Adrian sniffed the weather, looked around. "I don't like it. Its going to blow another gale – she'll be driven up again. Even if Graham's anchor holds her she'll crash herself on the rocks if the tide comes higher. If she's going to come off it will have to be now – get Archie on the VHF." I called up on Channel 8. "*Marie D'Or, Marie D'Or – Iskra.*" There was a long pause. "He's gone," I shouted. Then Archie's voice came loud and clear. They were back for the night in their berth alongside the pier a bit early because the weather threatened, on the point of going home. "Aye – we'll come in half an hour – another two minutes and we were gone home."

"Go and get Graham back – straight away." I ran across to the ferry terminal where the bicycles were. It would take me a good ten minutes to get to Graham's house, another few minutes to get back if I found him. We needed him, with his punt, to get the big anchor up and pass the line to the *Marie D'Or*. It was already past high water. The ferry was in – Vie was there, seeing off some visitors. "Vie take me to Graham's house – quick. We've got to get *Iskra* out now, before it starts blowing again. We need Graham – the tide'll be gone in minutes."

Vie caught the tone of urgency. She didn't hesitate – her

visitors were bundled out of the car, pecked on the cheek goodbye. She drove like the wind up through the village, past the store. Mrs. McSporran saw us flash by. Graham was frying fish for his tea. "Graham – Adrian says we've got to get her off now – before it starts blowing. Archie's on his way round from the pier. We need the punt to get the anchor." Graham thought for a moment, wrinkled brow, a look of appraisal round his seaman's eyes. "Aye – Adrian may be right – he may be right an' all." Graham dropped everything, we raced back to the cove in his car, together we brought the punt round, Graham set out to recover the anchor.

Adrian was on board as I rowed out with the rubber dinghy, I saw the *Marie D'Or* already coming round the point into the bay, white water curling round her bow. John Martin was on the shore now – the word had got around. News travels like lightning in Gigha. Adrian had not been idle – he and Wendy had laid out ropes on both sides of *Iskra*, two from for'ard and two from aft. "We'll have to steer her as she comes," he said, "by heaving on the ropes – you aft, me for'ard. She's still got to come round two corners." We spoke to Archie on VHF, Graham had lifted the anchor, passed the rope to the trawler's blunt stern. With the VHF we guided Archie to the right position. *Iskra* was still heeling a good 15°. I found it hard to believe that she could be moved by a tow when she was so hard aground, even if no rocks were in her way.

Everything was ready. Adrian said, "All right – tell him to start pulling." I glanced at my watch. The tide had gone for an hour yet the water was holding up, rising if anything. Out of the corner of my eye I saw Wendy and John on the shore. They had found a piece of stick, had stuck it on the edge of the shore as a tide gauge. Graham was rowing ashore with the punt. Archie started pulling gently so as not to jerk the tow line. We watched it slowly take the strain, the parts of the cradle firmly round *Iskra*'s hull – we adjusted the lines to the deck to make sure the rope had a fair lead. As the strain increased the cradle nestled itself round the hull, most of the strain on the stern post which was best able to withstand it. We saw a puff of black smoke from the *Marie D'Or*'s exhaust, heard the even beat of her powerful engine.

The strain increased, the heavy tow line began to tighten and lift – no movement from *Iskra*. The engine noise increased its pitch, another puff of black smoke, we saw the trawler's stern settle in the water – still no movement. We were tense, watching, silent. The noise rose again, now the ropes were squeezed thin with strain, the heavy tow line almost clear of the sea. The *Marie D'Or*'s stern bit deep, her big screw churning the water into white froth, the rope like an iron bar. Archie gave her the last of the throttle, the noise rose – it seemed to fill the cove with throbbing energy, black smoke poured from her funnel, the tow rope came clear of the sea, we saw it swinging gently, streams of water squeezing out of it. I looked over the side. *Iskra* was quivering as if charged with electric energy, she gave an imperceptible jump, a shake like an animal in pain. I looked at Adrian on the bow – he had felt it, "she's moving."

In a moment she gave another shake and then another – now we could see her moving against the shore. She was coming up now, only a slight list, she was moving faster.

"Archie," I shouted into the VHF, "Ease up – stop towing." Like a greyhound out of a trap she came free of the bottom and bounded ahead. Adrian heaved feverishly on his starboard line, I heaved on my port line. She slithered round the first rock, I saw its wicked, serrated side flash past her bilge, inches clear. She was free, afloat now – moving straight for the next rock – nothing would stop her. We heaved on the opposite lines. Archie had stopped towing but she carried her way – with no rudder we couldn't turn her in time, she ran helter-skelter into it, her bow slid up and she was stuck. Adrian came aft. She had moved so far ahead that my port line was now leading aft, straight over her stern, only two or three feet of it left. We lay on it together. We pulled until we thought our backs would break. "Oh no," I said, "not now for God's sake." We gave an extra heave, a last desperate effort. Quite suddenly she slid back, we fell in a heap on the deck –

she was clear again. The rock was smooth and had allowed her forefoot to slide away. Pure luck.

We spoke to Archie – asked him to move the *Marie D'Or* over to port. Then he started to tow again slowly, slowly. She was out of it, she was alive, she was moving under us as she always moved, the resolute, positive motion which is her hallmark. At first we couldn't believe it. We looked ashore. Wendy and Graham were side by side, Wendy jumping up and down like an excited child. Adrian and I shook hands, embraced on *Iskra*'s bridge deck. Archie towed us gently to the buoy – we made her fast with chain. Archie let go the tow line and the *Marie D'Or* went off with a cheery wave. We couldn't believe it. The wind was picking up – the makings of a new gale from the south-east.

8

Hard Choices

Wendy and Graham walked slowly back to Graham's car parked by the ferry ramp. It had been a traumatic hour. She had watched, unbelieving, as *Iskra* began to move hesitantly ahead. She knows how heavy *Iskra* is, how we can never shift her once she gets herself aground until the tide comes up. She knows that towing from another vessel is usually less effective than heaving from a fixed point on the shore, especially with a powerful tackle and eight men pulling. The *Marie D'Or* must be a very powerful vessel indeed. "Aye, she is," Graham said. "She's got a massive diesel engine in her." Wendy had watched with dismay as *Iskra* ran against the rock, had breathed again when she came off. The emotional switchback had left her exhausted. "Thank God its over," she said as she saw Adrian and me embrace on *Iskra*'s bridge deck. She looked at the tide gauge she and John had positioned by the edge of the shore. It had started to run out fast – in the last ten minutes the water seemed to have gone down by as many inches. It was as if the tide had held itself up especially for *Iskra*. Graham said, "Now ye'll be moving on to the job of getting her repaired. The best yard hereabouts is at Crinan, and that's a good twenty miles off."

As they drove up the road Wendy said, "There's only one disappointment – the Dolphin – *Iskra*'s figure-head under her bow – its gone. Frank was fond of him – thought he brought good luck." Graham stopped the car. "Figure-head?," he said, "Dolphin? Carved out of wood? – I saw something floating close to the shore beside my boat this morning." He turned the car, went back to where his boat lay. In the failing light they searched round the water's edge. At first they found nothing. Further up a small creek Graham saw something – a piece of wood, painted grey and black, he pointed. "That's him – that's Frank's Dolphin." The excitement bubbled out of her. My Dolphin was sitting by the edge of the creek, a bit shame-faced, his head turned down, his rounded forehead with the black dorsal giving away his hideout. Wendy picked him out of the mud. He was missing his tail, a sorry figure of a shipwreck survivor. They looked round again along the shore and in the next creek. Sure enough, cast up against the shore was half a tail. The other half had gone.

Adrian and I pumped *Iskra* dry when Archie had gone, waited for an hour, watching the bilge, trying to see where it was coming in. There was a leak up for'ard where she had run against the last rock, another at the top of her stern post, it was coming in fast along the seams on both sides of the patch. The lead tingle itself was keeping most of the water out. We could see a lot of damage along her starboard side, some of her frames appeared to be broken – it was a miracle she stayed afloat. We judged it safe to leave her. "I'll come back after supper, if necessary I'll stay aboard all night." She was high out of the water without her ballast and her gear. It was blowing hard now. We climbed into the rubber dinghy, rowed to the jetty by Catriona's café, walked to the waiting room to get the bikes, rode home to John's house.

There was a roaring wood fire in the living room, Wendy was cooking supper. We warmed our feet by the fire, talked round and over and about the day's happenings and what the next move should be – how were we to get her repaired? "I'm going to have a bath and change my clothes," I said. I went into the bedroom. It was a small room – John's spare, for his daughter when she came to stay. There were two single beds in it. In one of them, his head peering out over the bedclothes, his big grin spread across his visage, was my Dolphin. I let out a great shout. "You bloody Dolphin," I shouted. "You jumped ship – by God I'm glad to see you back." I ran back to the kitchen – we all had a drink to celebrate. "Aye – he was nae the only one tae be thinking *Iskra* was finished," John said. It was true.

I rowed the dinghy back late in the evening – it would be disaster if *Iskra* sank at the mooring. It was blowing hard but by skirting round the shore I found some shelter. I could see her in the light of a shy moon, peeping through scudding cloud. She was still riding high. I grabbed the shrouds as the dinghy was swept past, hauled myself aboard. The water was slopping about the cabin, almost up to the bunks. She would go for the night, I reckoned – I'd have to get on board early in the morning. I pumped 300 strokes of the hand pump in the cockpit, rowed ashore with some difficulty through the gale and left the dinghy hauled up the shore by the boathouse. We slept sound and happy that night, my Dolphin in a corner of the room, a bit shame-faced.

The boatyard at Crinan, after some hesitation, said that they could take *Iskra* in for repair. Archie agreed to tow her to the yard on Sunday, when there was no fishing, provided the weather was reasonable. He would charge me the cost of running the ship and her crew for a day. I agreed it, hoping the insurance would pay. I wrote them another letter, told them that *Iskra* had been salvaged with no claim against her and that I had agreed a tow to Crinan for £400. We had already spoken to my nephew Richard and his wife Mary. I phoned them again with the good news and they agreed to hire a van to transport our gear from the waiting room. We ought to take *Iskra* to Craobh Haven, they thought, where there was a good shed with all facilities – no shipwrights but we could find someone to work on her. It was an attractive idea.

"Better to go to the yard," Adrian said, "they're professionals, are used to wooden boats, will have everything needed."

"If she was at Craobh," I countered, "we might be able to get David to come up and work on her. We could bring everything we needed from Maldon."

"It would drag on for months," he replied, "there would be endless delays, you'd end up by getting the job half done."

"It would probably be cheaper," I said. The argument went on more or less continually and with no conclusions reached.

The next day another Force 9 gale was blowing. Somehow I got on board early. There was a lot of water in her, it took me more than an hour to pump her dry. I spent most of the day on board, squaring up, pumping at intervals, cleaning and trying to pin down the source of the biggest leak. As far as I could judge it was for'ard. I made a makeshift repair to the engine exhaust, using empty tins and some exhaust bandage I had among *Iskra*'s stores and had left on board. It ran at first with no oil pressure but after a few minutes the needle on the gauge jumped up to its old level. In the afternoon I put on my life-jacket and set off for the shore. There was no question of rowing across the wind to the jetty – the gale was nearly as fierce as the one that put us on the rocks. I eased the dinghy downwind, keeping it head to the seas and progressing backwards. The surf was jumping up over the rocks again, the ferry ramp had combers breaking on it like Bondi Beach. As I got close I saw there was a calm patch beside Graham's boat, a line of surf between me and it. As I would expect, he had chosen his berth with great care. I put the dinghy to the surf and it leapt through in a rush of spray but I managed to get ashore without a ducking. Adrian was there to meet me, or pull me out of the sea whichever was required. Wendy had spent the day washing. Every room in John's house was now festooned with clothes, blankets, towels.

Vie asked us all to supper in her cottage, she is a sculptor, makes lovely things from bog oak and hardwood she finds on the island. She lives in a cottage down a lane towards the sea from John's house. She is a bundle of energy, has done a lot of sailing, knew of *Iskra*. She showed us her studio, showed us a slim, graceful otter she had created. She gave us a copy of her guide to Gigha, an eminently readable booklet with her own illustrations of birds, wild flowers and animals to be found on the island.

The argument about the repair dragged on. I said, "We could stay with Richard and Mary if she was at Craobh, they are quite close to the yard, then we could help with the work."

Adrian said, "how can you be so sure David's free to work

on *Iskra?* He's not on the 'phone – you can't ask him."

Vie said, "the Crinan yard's a good yard – they repair all the wooden fishing boats around here. They've got a good reputation."

It seemed impossible to reach agreement; there were valid arguments on both sides. With faultless logic Wendy stepped in. "We should have a spare day on Saturday before Archie can take her. Why don't we hire a car, or borrow a car and go and look at the Crinan yard, look at the shed in the marina at Craobh? Then we'll be able to decide." Like all great ideas, it was of a monumental simplicity. Mrs. McSporran told us that Seamus would let us have a car. "One of us will have to stay with *Iskra* unless we can stop her leaking," I said.

We still had one day to prepare *Iskra* and our gear for the next part of the voyage— either to Crinan or to Craobh Haven. It was a calmer day with some sunshine. Adrian cleaned the ballast with a stiff brush and detergent, re-stowed it on another rock. At high tide he and Graham ferried it out to *Iskra* in the punt, making three trips before it was all aboard. They piled it neatly on the side decks. I found some underwater cement I had carried on board *Iskra* ever since our voyage to Argentina. It is used for repairing holes or cracks in ferro cement boats, I once saw it used on a boat we met in Madeira which had run into a sleeping whale in the night. The dent in the hull still had hair from the whale's skin round the edges. He had repaired the hole at sea. I bought a packet when we came back home and now I found it tucked away behind a locker in the fo'c'sle. I thought it must have deteriorated in five years, mixed a small amount in an old tin to test it. It set like rock in minutes. The rest of the packet spread over the inside of the stem stopped the worst leak. We would be able to leave her.

We spent most of the day on board, stowing the ballast neatly in the bilge again, putting back the cabin floorboards which Adrian brought from the shore, floating the boom and the broken bowsprit on board to be taken wherever she went and making ready for the tow. "Pray for a fine day on Sunday,"

Adrian said, "she may not tow well without her rudder." Richard Fox, who owned the trawler we had run foul of, came on board. There was slight damage to his ship, he said, but nothing much. I told him if he wanted to make a claim he should write to me but I never heard from him. He said he would be able to tow *Iskra* with the trawler. He would charge us £75 to tow us to Crinan. I said I would let him know. Graham and Iain Wilkieson thought it was a bad option.

Mrs. McSporran had a message for us as we cycled past the post office. She handed me a slip of paper, written on it, Peter Mather and a telephone number in Ipswich. "You've to 'phone him," she said. I showed it to Wendy. "I can't think who it can be – the only Peter Mather I know keeps a boat on the east coast, in the River Deben. He can't possibly know where we are. I think it's a waste of time – we're busy."

Wendy said, "No – you must 'phone him. It might be important."

I telephoned from the boathouse. "Frank," a voice said, "I couldn't believe it – your letters were in my post this morning. I managed to get through to the post office – Mrs. McSporran. She knows everything – said you were on board *Iskra*, you would be coming for your lunch about now."

I was puzzled. "Why are you phoning me?"

"Frank – this is Guardian Insurance." It was my turn not to believe it – I had no idea where Peter worked.

Peter agreed Archie's price for the tow at once, said the company would give us every possible assistance and support. He was delighted that *Iskra* wasn't damaged beyond repair. "Most owners these days are only interested in the cash for a total loss. It's good to see an owner who really wants to save his boat."

I said, through a haze of disbelief, "Perhaps there are not so many boats like *Iskra*." A helpful and sympathetic insurance company would put the job of repairing her on a new footing. "If we wanted to," I said to Adrian, "this probably means that we could get our own people to work on *Iskra*."

"We'll see tomorrow," he said.

Wendy and I picked up Seamus's car in time for the early ferry, Adrian went on board and pumped – there wasn't as much water this time. He joined us just before the ferry left. The Sound was calm now, the island serene in the early sunshine, the passage we had come through, the red buoy, the wide bay mild and innocent. We drove the twenty odd miles to Crinan through beautiful country beside Loch Tarbert and Loch Fyne. We had our coffee and shortbread beside a blazing wood fire in Lochgilphead, arrived at the yard and looked around. It was a busy yard, boats laid up cheek by jowl in a long, narrow shed. There was a good chandlery, boat repairing under way. The place had an air of efficiency struggling against a lack of space. The labour charge was not cheap by the standards of the day. "Things are seldom cheap when they are good," Adrian said wisely.

They were not sure when they could start the job on *Iskra* – it would depend on the work load. We had a beer in the pub overlooking the canal locks, a view of islands and sea and a bold coastline. We were in a very beautiful place, a good place to be in.

"They've got everything there – they would certainly be able to do the job," Adrian said.

"They're a busy yard," I countered, "we would have to fit in with their regular work, the locals, quite rightly, would take precedence over us." I doubted whether we'd be allowed to work in the yard, certainly we would not be allowed to supervise. We drove on to Craobh Haven, another lovely road through woods, up and over hills, always glimpses of calm water.

We found Richard and Mary on board *Bumble Bee* in the marina. They had completed their last charter of the year, the boat soon to be hauled out for the winter. They showed us the shed – a spacious place with a high platform across one end for stowage, a planer, a band saw, vices, a bench grinder – everything to hand for working on boats except shipwrights.

"Almost all the boats here are fibreglass," Richard said, "there's really not much demand for wood working." We saw the director of the marina. Yes, he was agreeable for us to employ our own shipwrights. He would charge us a fixed sum per week for the shed. They could lift *Iskra* out on Sunday, as soon as we arrived, she would stand outside, be moved into the shed as convenient. It looked good – even Adrian thought so. "I'll 'phone David."

I telephoned our chandlery in Maldon as a first try, spoke to Louise, told her *Iskra* had been on the rocks in Scotland and was seriously damaged, that I needed to speak to David urgently. By chance, David was working in the next yard, she thought. She would go and find him as soon as she could leave the chandlery and bring him to the phone. We fixed a time for him to telephone the box in the marina. We all had lunch. "You can stay with us as long as she's in the yard," Mary said, "they are a nice lot. John Macinnes, the foreman, is really helpful." I waited in the 'phone box – it rang on the minute. I told David I thought there was work on *Iskra* for at least a month, possibly longer, told him about the shed. "It's clean, it's got a good, even floor, it's warm, dry." I had already spoken to one of the girls in the marina who could put him up, we would be there working with him. There was a pause, quite a long pause.

"I can come at the end of October."

"Great man." I arranged to pay him £2 an hour more than he was getting at present, it was still well below the rate in Crinan. Adrian said, "It won't be easy to make it work – you'll have to bring everything you need with you." We drove back to the island, caught the last ferry. We saw *Iskra* as we came up to the red buoy, I went on board and pumped her out.

We would be sorry to leave the island so soon. Everyone knew us, we had made friends, some good friends. Vie had composed a poem for *Iskra*:

> *"Sadly, Gigha's rocks haunt Iskra's bilge,*
> *Surely, like a phoenix she will rise again?*
> *From frustrated listing on a treacherous shore,*
> *To strive and drive and butt into the sea,*
> *Surging spume out of her way."*

We knew we hadn't had time to explore, to poke about the island's crags and crannies, to find out more about the springs that made the island tick. We knew for sure they were generous hearted, easily enlisted to what they saw as a worthwhile project. Everyone had helped us without stint and with no reward. Roddy refused payment for his work, John Martin would not allow us to pay for our keep. I sent him money to defray expenses when we got home. He thanked me for it, sent the cheque to the lifeboat. Graham wouldn't allow me to pay for the damage to his boat. Vie gave us invaluable help and support, Seamus loaned us a car almost for nothing, we paid for the petrol and the ferry, our helpers not only gave us their brawn but sometimes wise advice. They loaned us rope and gear which we couldn't otherwise have got. Mrs. McSporran was always ready to give us invaluable information on anything and everything in Gigha.

Life is not always easy on the island. It was owned by a Swiss Bank when we were first there. The laird, inspired by the wisdom of the times, had taken out a mortgage on the island, which he had invested in property. For as long as property was riding high, he rode high with it, at least on paper. When it all began to tumble, he tumbled down into bankruptcy. The bank then became the island's owner. It wasn't the first time a laird of Gigha had been made bankrupt. It happened to John McNeill in 1832. On balance, we were told, the bank was not a bad laird, leaving the islanders to carry on much as before. Now it was for sale again. No one knew what kind of laird the next one would be, a vital consideration because the laird wields power on a feudal scale. By virtue of owning the island he becomes the Baron of Gigha. He would own every house on the island, with the exception of those of a few islanders who were their own masters. He could vary the rents at will, he could give notice to quit with no legal hindrance, effectively, he ruled the island like a medieval baron but with few of the baron's responsibilities. Everyone waited in hope and some trepidation for the island to be sold and the new laird to come. John had worked for the old laird until his eclipse, now he worked at the fish farm. There wasn't much in the way of industry on the island and farming seemed to be at a standstill. There was a hotel, some tourism in the summer. The total number of inhabitants was 120.

The next day was bright, sunny, windless – another break *Iskra* pulled out of her hat. In a strong wind and a choppy sea, with no rudder and no means of steering, it would have been a slow, difficult business to tow her safely. Adrian and I rowed aboard early. By the time we had stowed the rubber dinghy, singled up the various ropes, chains and preventers to the buoy, the *Marie D'Or* came briskly round the red buoy into the Bay. Archie brought her gently alongside, we passed him the end of one of Graham's or Iain's long warps. We let go the buoy, Archie took the strain and *Iskra* moved out of Ardminish Bay. Wendy was standing on the shore waving, Graham was on board the *Marie D'Or*; he had come to see the business properly finished. The Sound was beautiful with warm, autumn sunshine, the island a radiant spangle of greens and soft browns over the placid blue sea. *Iskra* towed well at a steady 5 knots, finding for herself a position a few degrees on the *Marie D'Or*'s quarter. There was nothing for us to do but watch her, check the bilge and see that the tow-line was free of chafe. We gave the engine a good run to charge the batteries, gazed out at the spectacular Scottish scenery as the shore sped past. We passed the entrance to West Loch Tarbert which almost makes an island of the Kintyre peninsula. The neck of low land between it and East Loch Tarbert on the other side is no more than three quarters of a mile wide.

The peninsula is full of ancient history. At the end of the 11th Century King Magnus Barefoot of Norway established sovereignty over the Hebrides. He maintained that Kintyre was an island and therefore part of his domain. To prove it he had himself carried in his ship across from East to West Loch Tarbert. There are first century vitrified forts on the peninsula which may have formed defences long before the days of mortar and cement. Stone wall fortifications were subjected to intense heat, using brush wood as fuel on a breezy day so that the stones were fused together into a solid defence. They are found in Scotland, not in England or Wales. There are at least two on Kintyre, one at Carradale on the east coast and another near Clachan at the entrance to West Loch Tarbert.

In ancient times the peninsula was densely populated and forested all down the west side. There are the remains of two castles and a Cistercian Abbey founded in 1160. Dunaverty Castle, on a rock off the south of the Mull of Kintyre was the seat of the MacDonalds, Lords of the Isles. Robert Bruce found sanctuary there during his long wanderings in Kintyre before he fled to Rathlin Island where he found the famous spider. Around the year 560 A.D. St Columba landed from Ireland on the Mull on his way to Iona; with the help of a little imagination you can see his footprints burnt into the rock. The island of Sanda, close off-shore from the Mull, was a safe haven for the Viking longships. Flora MacDonald, who shielded Bonny Prince Charlie from the English after the Scots' disastrous defeat at Culloden, emigrated to North Carolina from Campbeltown in 1774, some thirty years after she helped the prince escape. The historical catalogue of the Kintyre peninsula is endless. It is one of the most scenic parts of the west of Scotland with splendid views on both sides from the high ridge down the centre. It was depopulated in the clearances, the crofts cleared, the people driven away to America and Australia.

The Sound narrowed towards the top, we passed the necklace of islands off the notorious tide race of Corryvreckan between Jura and Scarba and soon into the enclosed waters south of Shuna, the marina of Craobh Haven under our bow.

On Gigha Wendy collected up all our gear at the ferry terminal. We had in effect taken it over for a week – no one objected or complained, no item of our gear went missing although the place was open at all times. Wendy searched round the shore to make sure we had collected up all our belongings, made a separate pile of the gear that had been loaned to us. On the midday ferry Richard and Mary arrived with the hired Transit van. Everything was neatly packed in, the big rudder at the bottom, all our sails, ropes and gear, the cushions, mattresses and newly washed bedding and the myriad items that make of a boat a home. She said goodbye to John and Vie and anyone she found, the van was driven onto the 2 p.m. ferry and they drove to Craobh Haven. *Iskra* arrived at lunchtime, to be met by the yard launch. We hauled alongside the *Marie D'Or* to pass over the tow-line. I found a bottle of brandy in the locker, half a dozen mixed glasses and mugs.

"Here's wishing you luck," Archie said.

"Here's thanking you all," I said. "If it wasn't for you all there would be no *Iskra*." We shook hands all round, Graham, Archie, the *Marie D'Or*'s crew. "We'll bring her along for you to see in the spring." The *Marie D'Or* went off with a toot on her whistle.

9

Rebirth

With an abrupt shift, the direction of our efforts moved from one set of problems to another. As the *Marie D'Or* faded into the Sound of Jura everything changed. We had completed the easiest chapter of *Iskra*'s return to good health. The issues had been straightforward, our options limited by stark necessity. We had been guided by a single aim to which we had all directed our efforts, *Iskra* herself seemed to have helped us in every way she could, many cards had fallen out of the pack face up. We had been given the selfless help of people who had never known us, who owed us no obligation or loyalty. We could only assume that it was the workings in our favour of that timeless law of the sea which demands the giving of assistance in all circumstances to any vessel or mariner who meets misfortune. Now we were on our own, now our choices were wider and less easy to resolve, our options restricted by considerations outside *Iskra*'s survival. At least we had the job in our own hands and we had the insurance company on our side.

The launch towed *Iskra* into a concrete dock and in due course the travel lift arrived, its progress across the yard punctuated by stops and starts and shakes and swerves as if it was in the charge of a newcomer to the art of manipulating this monster. It was. It was manned by the two directors of the marina who had generously given up their Sunday to make sure *Iskra* was promptly lifted out. At length they managed to position the machine over *Iskra*, we helped them fasten the slings under her keel. The engine roared, an array of knobs and levers were pushed and pulled in turn until the right one was found and she was taken up on the aft sling. The Managing Director leaned out over the dock to secure the for'ard sling, the machine suddenly moved a fraction, the Managing Director plunged head first into the dock. Adrian hauled him out by one arm, restored to him his hat. He stood dripping and shivering, looked up to the other director at the controls. "We'll finish it," he said, grittily. "I'll get dry afterwards." The tide was going – it wouldn't wait. Adrian fastened the forward sling and *Iskra* rose up out of the sea, first one end and then the other, to reveal her twisted keel timber, her shattered forefoot, her scarred and broken bilge. The machine crawled unsteadily up into the centre of the yard, *Iskra* was set down on blocks. "We'll leave her in the slings for the night," both directors carried expressions of quiet triumph. "I don't believe John Macinnes thought we could do it."

Soon Richard and Mary and Wendy arrived in the transit van from Gigha. We off-loaded the rudder, the steering vane, the broken bowsprit, the sails, all the running rigging and blocks we had used in *Iskra*'s salvage, stowed them all on the balcony of the shed. The shed was empty except for two small plastic boats hauled out along one side. *Iskra* would fit in nicely, with plenty of space round her, plenty of room for working under cover. It was an ideal spot. The marina had been built some five years previously; it had run into financial difficulties, had been forced into liquidation and eventually bought by a company headed by our two director friends. John Macinnes was the yard foreman, we would see him when we came in the morning. Our winter cover and the wooden struts that Adrian had sent from home were in a corner of the shed. *Iskra* seemed to be the only wooden boat in the place. Apart from the shed there wasn't much to help us – a small chandlery, showers, a nearby pub. The marina had a half finished look about it, it was clear the money had run out but the pontoons looked as though they had been well designed and constructed. It is in a fine position – an outlook over Asknish Bay, enclosed by islands, narrow passages between where the tide runs. Behind, the land rises sharply to a thickly wooded ridge running way to the south towards Jura. It would be a wonderful place to walk – one day when we had time.

I had negotiated a fixed rent of £250 per week for all the time *Iskra* was in the shed. There would be no surcharge on the shipwrights' work, no extras for electricity or for the storage of our gear on the balcony. If the yard men helped us, there would be a charge. On the basis of my 'phone call to David I fixed a day for *Iskra* to be moved from the freestanding in the yard into the shed – the last Saturday in October. It would give us a month at home to make preparations. David would arrive on the Sunday. I had told him to allow four weeks for the job but when Adrian and I saw the extent of the damage we began to doubt this time scale. "We'll have to see what David thinks." We met John Macinnes and the boys working in the yard on Monday morning. *Iskra*'s mast was lifted out and slung from the rafters of the shed, John moved her smoothly across the yard with the travel lift – he was the real master of the machine. It behaved for him like an obedient dog. Adrian and I built up the wooden structure for the cover, every moveable thing that remained in her was stowed in the shed. Adrian went back to Essex by train the next day to get on with his business. All I could say to him was, "thanks – I couldn't have done it without you." I felt much more but the words were blocked off by a constraint outside my control. We shook hands and he went off.

We made a tentative arrangement for Bed and Breakfast for David with one of the marina's secretaries – we had an idea that we might hire a caravan so that Wendy and I wouldn't have to drive the twenty miles back and forth to Richard's house every day. When we left Craobh Haven for home we had the nucleus of a system for repairing *Iskra*. "At least the people in the marina are really nice," Wendy said. John Macinnes was a big fellow with ginger hair, broad shoulders, there was an engineer called Rob, and Tim who assisted John and another lad. They were all fascinated by the idea of having a wooden boat in the shed and wanted to help in any way they could. "I dinna see how ye'll fix her up in a month," John said.

It happened that there was a bus from Oban to London which passed Richard's door – it was cheaper and quicker than the train. We piled into it with a motley selection of gear, including *Iskra*'s tiller, nearly six feet long and the broken stub from the rudder head. David was appalled when we told him the extent of the damage. "I'll never do it in a month," he said, "I've got more work planned for the middle of December – I'll have to have help." The obvious person was Ariane who had worked with David on and off for a long time but she was employed by Arthur Holt in his yard at Heybridge Basin near Maldon. When I went to see Arthur, to ask him whether he would release her for a month, I realised Ariane Van Wageringen was a much in demand lady. "I can't," he said, "I'm relying on her for a score of jobs."

I reported Arthur's refusal to David. "Leave it to me – I'll try." Inside a week it was agreed that Arthur would release Ariane for four weeks. They would come to Craobh together in David's car.

I gave the broken tiller and the measurements of *Iskra*'s bowsprit to Ian Danskin, another Maldon shipwright, who agreed to make replacements in time for David and me to take to Scotland on the roofs of our respective cars. We estimated how much copper we would need, I bought it in sheets, ready to load into my mini estate car. *Iskra*'s planks are screwed to the oak frames with bronze screws. I had extracted one from the broken plank, together with a sample of the copper roves that fasten the planks to the steamed oak timbers. We bought a good supply. We made lists of everything we could think of that we would need – it might be difficult and time wasting to get things locally.

John Macinnes gave me the name of a local surveyor who was used to working with wood. I spoke to him on the 'phone before we left Scotland. As it happened he was in the area – he agreed to come over at once so that we could meet him before we went home. By another chance James McIlraith was the surveyor chosen by the insurance company. He turned out to be young, knowledgeable and sympathetic to our method of getting *Iskra* repaired. He would survey her in a few days and send the report without delay to the company, together with an estimate of cost. I told him in detail what had happened – he knew the waters round Gigha, understood it all, with a sad shake of his head for an old wooden boat. *Iskra* was looking after herself again. The report came as promised within ten days. It was an excellent report, giving a clear picture of the extent of the damage and a shrewd indication of difficulties we might run into. David studied it in detail. "It's going to be a job to get it finished, even with two of us."

Once the insurance company understood that we were anxious to get the job done as quickly and as cheaply as possible they gave us a free hand to do it in our own way – within the limits of the surveyor's estimate for the work which came to £9,000. The insured value was only £12,500. I was conscious that this figure was far too low – I had put it up year by year but never by enough to take account of the escalation in boatyard costs and the escalation in the value of classic boats. I half expected them to cut a percentage off my claim to compensate for this but they didn't. I made a point of keeping them well informed, by frequent written progress reports, from the moment the accident took place and I believe this may have had some bearing on their sympathetic attitude.

I negotiated an hourly rate for David and Ariane of £9.50 per hour, which at that time was well above what they were currently earning. They would be paid a living allowance of £12.50 a day each to defray the cost of the Bed and Breakfast. David would be paid expenses for driving his car to Scotland, his petrol and a small lump sum for wear and tear on the car. I would pay them each week, I would send an invoice to the insurance company with receipts for their wages and for every item I had bought for the repair. The company would send me a cheque by return. I made it clear that the whole operation would depend on these weekly cheques being promptly paid otherwise I would rapidly run out of money. I told them that Wendy and I would both work with the shipwrights, as far as our limited skills permitted, and that we would not charge our time. They agreed all my suggestions. We wondered what would have happened if we had not had a friend at court. "I think it would have been the same," Peter said, "they'll always help someone who is trying to keep the claim as low as possible."

Another stroke of luck fell our way before we left home for Craobh Haven at the end of October. We had been uneasy about the arrangements for the shipwrights to stay in Bed and Breakfast. Even if we gave them a snack at lunchtime they would still have to buy their evening meal. There was nowhere to eat in the evening at Craobh Haven, the Bed and Breakfast lady thought she would not be able to do it, they would have to drive at least 10 miles to the nearest pub, which would be expensive, tiring and time wasting. David didn't much take to the idea of a caravan – he doesn't like cold weather. There were houses to let around the marina but they were far too expensive, even in winter. Then Richard heard of a much cheaper holiday home up the hill and along an unmade track behind the marina. It was beside a riding stable and was let to horsey people in the summer. I spoke to the owner on the 'phone. He wanted £100 a week but in the end he accepted £60. "I'll take it." We hadn't seen it, hoped it would be possible. David and Ariane agreed to the plan, with some reservations I believe.

"Will it be warm?" David asked.

"I don't know – I'll buy a ton of coal."

We agreed that we would purloin both their living allowances, in return Wendy would provide full board and all expenses for all of us.

Wendy and I drove our Mini to Scotland a week before David and Ariane to get everything ready for them to start work. The mini was loaded to its marks, the roofrack piled high with stores and Ian Danskin's beautifully laminated new tiller, to the exact pattern of the old one. There must be no waste of time if they were to be finished in a month. John Macinnes moved *Iskra* into the shed, we took the cover off and started to strip out the accommodation on the starboard side. Everything had to be dismantled down to the bare hull, the pieces numbered and marked so that we would be able to see how it all went back. As we exposed the bare hull we began to get an idea of the real extent of the damage. There was more than I had imagined. We stripped off the broken sheets of copper on the outside of the hull, saving any that could be used again, took a dozen vital measurements, as instructed by David, 'phoned them back to him. He and Ariane would drive up on Saturday and Sunday.

We stayed in Richard and Mary's house in Connel, drove to the yard every day. The Scottish countryside was ablaze with autumn colour, all scarlet and gold and subtle browns, the vistas of forested hills and valleys and lakes and lochs along the quiet roads as beautiful as any we had seen. On Saturday we took possession of our cottage. It was a jewel, perched on a high embankment over the loch, dazzling white clouds, patches of blue, sometimes black clouds sailing across a screen of islands and seas. Far away across the Firth of Lorne the snow-covered mountains of Mull glistened in the sun. Beyond the riding stables which were beside the cottage was the big house, Lunga, a pretentious Scottish mansion of Victorian vintage. It was a mock baronial hall with an immense fireplace, enormous, tall rooms. It was owned, I believe, by the Dowager Duchess of Argyll – at least the Dowager Duchess was occasionally in residence. She divided her time between Lunga and a flat in Paris and another residence somewhere else in Scotland. We never met her but we were aware of her presence. A piper came to Lunga early every morning in full regalia, paced the lawn beneath her window so that she was woken early each day to the strains of his mournful and haunting melodies.

The cottage was built of stone, with a big room downstairs embracing a kitchen and a dining alcove, a fireplace across one end, easy chairs, bookcases, the stairs up one side. Above were bedrooms, a bathroom, airing cupboard. There was a pile of logs in the yard, a coal house. The track up the hill was too rough and muddy for our Mini. We took it up once, with a load of Wendy's kitchen gear from *Iskra* to supplement what was in the cottage and our food shopping for the first week. Afterwards, we always left the car in the yard. It was too beautiful to waste the pleasure of walking. We bought coal, made a roaring fire to warm the place through. Ariane and David arrived as planned on Sunday afternoon with another car load of stores, the new bowsprit and planks of larch on the roof. They thought it was a fine shed, they liked the cottage. Wendy made our first supper, we were set to go.

As we emerged sleepily in the morning the sombre music of the pipes echoed round the woods, thrown back and forth among the mountains. "That'll wake you up for the day's work," the shipwrights smiled wanly. We were in the yard when John opened the shed at 8.00. David and Ariane had a thorough look at *Iskra*. There were three broken 4 inch oak frames, eight of the steamed timbers between were broken, one of her pitch-pine planks was smashed in, another badly scored. For'ard, where she had mauled herself on the trawler, two planks were broken, the covering board split, the toerail smashed, the caulking shaken out of the topsides. The massive oak timber forming her forefoot was torn away exposing a twisted keel bolt. The wood keel itself and the iron keel under it had been forced out of true – all the keel bolts would have to be replaced, the engine would have to be moved. The rudder pintles were broken or wrenched free of the hull, both her 50 gallon water tanks had been split open. It was a miracle she had stayed afloat, David thought. The pitch-pine she was planked with is a remarkable wood. Clearly it had given with the impact, the planking had all been forced in, breaking the ribs and timbers, it had then sprung out again resuming its former shape. The damaged plank would have to be replaced by a plank of larch, butted fore and aft to the existing plank. It was sad. Every other plank in *Iskra* runs the full length of the hull. The copper sheathing had remained more or less intact, had kept the caulking in place and most of the water out. It was a formidable programme of work for two shipwrights to complete in four weeks.

They started work without delay. They seemed to know instinctively which of them would do which job and went about it with no needless discussion. Ariane started work on the new plank, David went straight to the keel bolts. *Iskra's* planks are fastened to the frames with bronze screws, riveted with copper roves to the timbers. Only one section of one plank was to be replaced – the one next to it would have a graving piece let in.

It wasn't long before David ran into difficulties. The old keel bolts were badly rusted in, two of them seemed to be distorted. At some time in *Iskra's* life, probably when the engine was fitted in the 1940s, a massive false keelson had been superimposed on the existing keelson. David thought this must have been done to strengthen her aft part to take the weight of the engine and to stop her drooping aft. This timber, a piece of 6 inch oak, covered the heads of three keel bolts. David had to drill it, exactly in the right place to expose the heads of the old bolts. The engine had to be moved first, using a chain hoist to lift it clear. The old bolts had to be drilled out, which took him many days of careful work. Like many boats of her time, *Iskra's* bilges were filled with cement, covering some of the keel bolt heads, making it difficult to locate them.

Wendy and I were despatched off to a boatyard in Kilmelford, five miles along the road to Oban, to get the new keel bolts made up. John Macinnes told us they had a good engineering shop. At first the yard's owner Nevin Blackwood, was slightly suspicious and not inclined to be helpful. I believe he suspected David of being something of a cowboy, coming to Scotland and taking work away from the locals. When he saw David's precise drawings of what he wanted and heard our description of the job in hand, he softened. I always took Wendy with me on these forays to find what we needed. She is a great confidence builder. In fact Nevin made all the ironwork efficiently and quickly, also the bronze fittings for the rudder, a new propeller shaft, a refurbished stern gland

and half a dozen other vital parts. All his work was excellent. We found in Scotland that once people knew what we were about and how we were trying to achieve it they did everything they could to help us.

I spent hours telephoning on the balcony of the shed while Wendy was kept busy stripping copper off *Iskra*'s bottom, plugging the nail holes with splines of wood, scraping the paint from the topsides and supplying us with meals. We needed more timber, oak for the keel and for the stem which I located in a Glasgow timber yard. It was despatched by express carrier to Craobh. I 'phoned orders to a firm in Suffolk known to David for more screws and nails and nuts and washers and bolts and copper roves, to be sent express. I 'phoned all over Scotland for unseasoned oak for the steamed timbers. It was impossible to buy it – the kiln dried oak which was available would not do because it cannot be steam bent. I was at my wit's end – the time was drawing close when Ariane would need it for the timbers.

Wendy and I went shopping in Oban once a week for provisions. Richard told me of a little boatyard in the town where I might get the oak, a boat builder now no longer building wooden boats. David Currie had no oak timbers but I found in his yard four oak tree crooks which would do for the frames. I paid him £70.50 for them all and loaded them into the Mini. Time ticked on and I still had no oak fit for steaming. In desperation I 'phoned the Crinan boatyard. "Not a hope old chap," Ben Laycock told me. "You can't buy it – no one builds wooden boats in Scotland. Everything's laminated these days." It was John Macinnes who came up with the answer. "There's a wee saw mill in Kilmelford," he told me. "Harry Clark may be able to help you." We went to find Harry at once.

The boys in the yard were fascinated with the work on *Iskra*. They had never seen a female shipwright before and were amazed at the speed she worked at and the magical way large pieces of oak became integral parts of *Iskra*, fitting so exactly that you couldn't pass a cigarette paper between the joints.

The work was organised among us so that the shipwrights did nothing but work which was beyond our skills. Every minute of their time had to be saved. I had a horror of coming to the end of it with the job half completed.

Wendy produced lunch every day on the balcony and a steady flow of mugs of tea which is a vital lubricant for shipwrights. She disappeared in the afternoons, toiled up the hill, lit a roaring fire and prepared our evening meal. With her economic management the living allowance fed us all and stretched to a bottle of wine every night. Between running messages, telephoning, fetching and carrying and sweeping up I spent my time burning off the topside paint which had not been done for years. The word had got around about the happenings in the shed at Craobh Haven, a stream of visitors and watchers dropped in to see how the job was progressing. Michael Leng, who had just started the Alba Smokehouse in nearby Lochgilphead came and asked us for oak wood shavings for smoking salmon. We collected it in bags when David and Ariane machined the massive timbers for the keel. He gave us a side of salmon in exchange. It was royal food for shipwrights – we were, all of us, living the life of Riley.

I found Harry Clark by the sawmill off the road to Kilmelford, sunk in the forest, a few stone barns, an ancient mill driven by an ancient diesel engine, under a dim shed. It was what the Scots call a driech day with a light, soaking, misty rain. "Och no," he said, "we've had nothing like that for years, at all." He sat in silence on the edge of the mill for a minute. We explained why we needed wet oak, how long the timbers were, what size they must be cut to. He shook his head, slowly. We were on the point of going away but something held me back. We stood looking at the ground, shuffling from foot to foot for another minute of so. Then Harry said, "Commander Campbell-Gibson – he lives over there, just across the road. His son had a big oak in his garden – it blew down a few months ago." We found the Commander just leaving his house. Yes, he might sell the tree provided it could be taken out of his son's garden without destroying paths or flower beds. The branches had already been taken, only the main trunk was left, but it was a big one.

We walked up the lane from his house, past an oak wood. The Commander was knowledgeable about trees and gardens. The wood, he told us, was coppiced and managed so that the flora resembled ancient woodland. He had a rare orchid growing in his garden which looked like a white hyacinth. It takes seven years to germinate, needs two kinds of fungi and exactly the right humidity and the right soil. It sets no seed and has no bulb and it only grows in the Commander's garden and in one other place in Devon. It is called Cephalanthera Longefolia. They had tried to transplant it to the Scottish National Trust's Ardaine Gardens next door, but it wouldn't take. He told us how the orchid had been identified. One day the Commander saw a man wandering in his wood – he challenged him, asked him what he was doing. The man turned out to be a well known naturalist who had gone into the wood because he had noticed some rare wild flowers. The Commander showed him the orchid and he identified it.

The oak had been a mature tree, two, possibly three hundred years old. The Commander agreed to sell it for the standard price for oak, he did a rapid calculation and came up with a figure of £180. I said, "As far as I can tell I would like to buy it but I must get the shipwright to look at it."

David said, "We'll send Ariane – she knows about trees." We found the Commander the same afternoon and all walked up the lane to look at the oak. I introduced Ariane.

"I thought you were going to bring your shipwright to look at it," he said.

"Ariane is the shipwright."

I pardoned him for his astonishment. It would be hard to find anyone who looks less like a shipwright than Ariane, in spite of her bobbed hair and the foot-rule sticking out of her pocket. Her pale blue eyes, slim figure and her charm shine through the jeans and the old blue sweater. Scottish men are not used to woman shipwrights. None of them really believed it until they started talking to her. The depth of her

Scarred forefoot.

Stripping damaged copper.

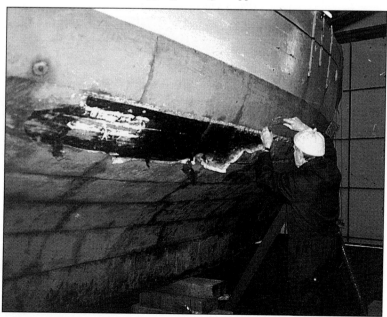

The Commander's oak.

Chain saw to the rescue.

New ribs and timbers.

Shipwrights and friend.

New into old.

Finishing touches.

knowledge is impressive – the Commander was as bowled over as the next. It gave me amusement to take her round on these jobs. She looked at the tree with minute attention, scraping away the mould and damp from the exposed grain. After a learned discussion with the Commander about the physical properties of oak she found what she expected would be a slight flaw which she pointed out to him. But she was pleased enough with it, "It'll do," she said. The deal was concluded, we settled on £125.

As we walked back I saw a mechanical digger working in a wood by the path. It had an extending lifting mechanism on the back, a scoop on the front. Colin Clark, no relation to Harry, owned the digger and worked as a free-lance on forestry jobs and anything else that came his way. The lift on the back would bring the trunk out without damaging the garden. He would do it the same afternoon. It was Saturday – we needed the oak on Monday. Harry would cut it on the sawmill to a size small enough to put on the saw in the shed and then Ariane and David could cut the ribs, 1½ ins x 1¾ ins. It was just in time – Ariane would be out of work on Monday without it. We were in high spirits when we all had lunch on the balcony.

John said, "Ye'll be pleased just now, with the way it's worked out."

David said, "There's more timber than we can possibly use."

I 'phoned Ben Laycock at Crinnan. "Would you like to buy some wet oak for steaming? I've just bought a tree." He gave me the sizes he would like, I charged him £50, he would come and collect it.

Another snag was to stand in our way before we got the oak for *Iskra*'s timbers. Wendy and I went to the sawmill after lunch in time to see the trunk arrive, nicely balanced on the scoop of the digger. With a skill that reminded me of John's handling of the travel lift, Colin manoeuvred the digger round, transferred the trunk to the crane and lifted. It was so heavy that it almost lifted the feet of the digger off the ground. Slowly the crane stretched itself out and under the shed, the log was gently positioned over the line of rollers ready to slide into the saw. "Stop," Harry shouted. "It's a wee bit big and a wee bit heavy – the saw will nay take it." It was clear. The trunk sat heavy on the rollers, too heavy to move. Harry's "I canna do it." was final. Colin lifted the trunk clear, we all sat down and thought.

I said, "What about a chain saw?" without much hope. "Aye," Harry said, "there's a man in Kilmartin with a big chain saw." We went at once, it was another ten miles past the marina and along the road the other way. Kilmartin is a village straggling the road to Lochgilphead. I asked in the craft shop just off the road.

"Yes," John Thornton said, "I have a two handed chain saw that will cut it. I can do it at the end of next week."

"No good. I need it tomorrow."

"Not a hope – I'm sorry." I told him the reason for our urgency.

"I know a man in Lochgilphead who has a saw like mine – he might help you."

I used John's 'phone – Steve Hunter was in. He thought for a minute. "You only just caught me – I was just going out of the door. I'll do it tomorrow morning at 9.00."

Whether it was the helpfulness of everyone we met in Scotland, or perhaps just the power of good luck, everything seemed to be working in our favour. Invariably, if someone couldn't do what we asked, they would know of someone else who could, or of someone who would tell us who could. Wendy always says "It's better to be born lucky than rich."

We were more than half way through our time limit. Thanks to careful management there was enough money left every week from the housekeeping purse for us to have dinner on Saturday at the Cuilfail Hotel in Kilmelford. We were known by now, there was always keen discussion in the bar on the progress of our project. We would sit over dinner on Saturday, discuss the week's work and plan the next week. David said, "Time's getting short, there's still a lot of work to be done. We'll start half an hour earlier, start working on

Sunday." I had insisted from the beginning that there should be a day off on Sunday but now David decided they would work at least half a day. Ariane had made and fitted the new frames, she was getting on well with the planks in the topsides and the damage to the foredeck. The massive piece of oak in the stem had been fashioned and set in place, to the astonishment of the people in the marina, but the job wasn't even half finished.

The image of a tough shipwright which Ariane likes to show to the world was dented one Sunday when we all walked over to the Galley of Lorne. Half way through the lane to Ardfern we came across a stray kitten, hungry and dejected, crouched under an empty caravan. Ariane carried it back to the cottage, fed it, played with it. The kitten became a part of the household.

David had been delayed by *Iskra*'s obstinate old keel bolts. They had finally yielded to his long reach drill but it had taken time. The bronze work for the rudder and the new stern tube and propeller shaft had been made but not yet put in place, there was the copper to be put back, a hundred other jobs. Wendy and I had nearly finished burning off the old paint on the topsides, she had varnished the new bowsprit, hammered in splines until her arms were fit to fall off. The insurance company was paying up every week against my invoices, keeping the whole merry-go-round going with cash. I sent them a progress report every week with the week's invoice. The most important job now was the timbers.

At 9.00 sharp on Sunday Steve Hunter and a helper arrived in a Land Rover with the chain saw. It was a complicated piece of equipment, all stainless steel and alloy, made in Sweden. Two motors, one each end, drove a horizontal chain stretched between steel pillars, all slung on an alloy frame so that it could be positioned over any job. The trunk was chocked up off the ground, an aluminium ladder placed on top of it to act as a guide for the first cut, the two motors started and the saw was moved along the ladder, slicing off the top of the trunk. They made four cuts, reducing the trunk to a square section of clean timber, the job took less than an hour. Then Steve stopped. "We'll leave it to Harry now," he said, "the sawmill has a thinner blade than our chain. It'll make a more accurate cut and you won't waste so much good oak in shavings." I paid Steve £50 and he and his mate went off. The shavings were in a thick mound on the ground. Mindful of the smoked salmon Wendy scooped them into plastic bags. Now the oak ran through the mill easily, Harry cut the sections for *Iskra*'s ribs, David took them to the shed on the roof of his car ready for work in the morning. The job was finished by lunchtime, the timber for the Crinnan yard put on one side.

The surveyor came to see the job every week, expressed himself pleased with progress. "You could save money and time by doubling up the timbers," he said, "instead of taking the old ones out." David looked at him with a raised eyebrow but said nothing. "It wouldn't be a proper job," he said to me afterwards. The surveyor recommended an extra keel bolt at the stern – David drilled through the two foot of wood keel and the bolt was put in. Ariane removed each of the broken timbers with meticulous care not to damage the planking, making a scarf at the bottom of each one so that the new timber could be married to the old, removing the old roves and rivets so that the new ones could use the same holes in the planking. She machined the new timbers through the planer while David and I improvised a steam box. John Macinnes found us an old piece of cast iron pipe lying about in the yard, long enough and wide enough to accept three of the timbers at a time. We fastened it a few feet above the ground to a couple of iron stands. Tim found us an odd piece of rubber pipe we poked into the top of an empty five gallon paint drum, the whole affair joined together with a pair of Wendy's rubber gloves. The drum was filled with water and boiled up on the yard's diesel heater. Soon a wisp of steam then a steady flow poured through the pipe. The first timber was put in, the second half an hour later and then the third, each one numbered with a small piece of knotted rope tied to the end. The timbers must steam for two hours, no more, no less or they will break as they bend to the exact shape of the hull.

It wasn't an easy job because *Iskra* has a heavy bilge stringer, a single length of oak from for'ard to aft laid over the frames. The timbers must be forced up behind the stringer and pressed to the side of the hull while they are still hot from the steamer, then fastened with clamps exactly in the line of the old timber, with Ariane's scarf slotting into place and glued. In half an hour the hot oak will set forever in its new shape. The new plank had been left out until last to give a hole in the hull. I was positioned at the steam box, Ariane and David inside *Iskra*. She had been cleared out inside ready to receive the timbers. David chalked on the floor beside the steamer the time each timber must be put into the steamer and the time it must be taken out. The keel bolts had been finished, David's hole in the false keelson filled with a piece of oak made and shaped in John Thornton's craft shop, the engine was back in position.

When the two hours were up I slid the first hot timber out of the steamer. They were 8 ft long, 1⅝ ins wide x 1½ ins thick. I passed it through the hole the right way round, David took it and he and Ariane slid it from amidships under the bilge stringer and up the side of the hull to the top, bending it to follow the exact curve of *Iskra*'s hull, forcing it hard against the planking. The scarfs at the bottom matched perfectly. They tapped the timber gently into place so that it lay correctly over the rivet holes and it was clamped and fastened. I slid a new timber into the steam box, half an hour later the next one was passed in. It took five hours non-stop work to get all the timbers in – two were broken because of a flaw in the wood. The shipwrights worked almost without speaking, methodically, unhurriedly but always certain and accurate in their movements. Under my eyes, *Iskra* assumed her shape and form. In five hours she was transformed from a broken hulk, all sagging and weak and hopeless, to the rigid, well knit, robust structure I had always known. Her vitality and strength were returned to her. For me and for Wendy it was a triumphant day's work.

Ariane slipped in the new plank, already prepared and ready to drop into place, fastened it to the new frames and timbers, caulked and filled all the planking along the starboard side. David fastened the new sacrificial timber along the bottom of the wood keel, hung the rudder on its new pintles, connected the new propeller shaft to the engine, began to piece together the old copper we had saved and recover the bottom with new, folding and fastening it neatly round the stern post. The copper is laid on thick brown paper, stuck to the hull with a generous layer of black varnish. We found that the paper we had brought would not absorb the black varnish – I was despatched to buy more, found it in a wholesale stationer's in Oban. We ran short of copper. I located some with an offset litho printer in Kilmartin. We needed one more week to finish. I wrote to Arthur Holt, Ariane spoke to him on the telephone. He relented. The marina allowed us to stay another week in the shed, we arranged one more week's rent for the cottage. David worked furiously to finish the copper sheathing, Ariane re-built the accommodation, fastening everything back into place just as it had been before. We bought flexible plastic inserts for the broken water tanks. One day, when we can afford it, we will have new ones – stainless steel instead of galvanised iron. Wendy finished varnishing the bowsprit, and Ariane put on the old ironwork. Between them they shipped it, with new, bronze chain plates which David had found in his store. We painted the topsides with seven coats, Rob, the marina's engineer, put in a new exhaust system for the engine.

She was finished. Wendy and I went round her with David and Ariane. We looked at every inch of her, inspected every job. We could find nothing that was not done to our satisfaction, that was skimped or half finished. Everyone came and looked at her, somehow the word got round that the job was completed. A stream of people we knew, some we didn't, came to see. Richard and Mary who had supported us and borne with us without complaint, John and Tim and Rob who had all helped us, the directors of the marina, Commander

Campbell-Gibson, fascinated to see the destination of his tree, Nevin who had made our iron and bronze work, Harry and Colin – a dozen others. She looked fine in her new paint, her new copper bottom, her bright varnish. *Iskra* seemed to preen herself, to swell up to her old proportions, the line of her hull as easy and sweet as ever, the lift of her bow as pretty, the fine run of her quarters with the same subtle grace. David and Ariane went off in David's old car, our broken bowsprit on the roof for me to make Wendy a garden seat one day when there is no boat work. We walked up to the cottage for the last time, said goodbye to Mary in the riding stables, looked at the spread of islands and rain and scudding cloud once more, packed our bags. In a last wander along the lane to Ardfern we found the owner of the caravan and restored her kitten to her. John moved *Iskra* out into the open again, we set up the struts for the cover, hauled it into place and tied it down. We loaded ourselves into our little car, drove the hundreds of miles to home. It had been a traumatic time. Neither of us could say we regretted it.

Orkney Islands

Iskra's Voyage Home

OUTER
HEBRIDES

Cape
Wrath • Scrabster
Kinloch-
bervie • Durness
*The
Minch*

Stroma
Duncansby Head
• Wick

58° N

Portree

Moray Firth • Fraserburgh

SKYE

SCOTLAND • Aberdeen

Tobermory

Dundee
*River
Tay*

MULL
Firth of Lorn

Glasgow

Jura

Edinburgh

St Abb's Head
• Berwick-upon-Tweed
• Farne Islands
• Amble

56° N

Gigha

*NORTH
SEA*

*Mull of
Kintyre*

ULSTER

E
I
R
E

Irish Sea

• Whitby

54° N

WALES

The Wash
Lowestoft
Southwold
Orford

ENGLAND

52° N

• Bradwell

N

50° N

English Channel

5° W

0°

10

Round the Top

More by chance and expediency than by design we had hit on what I now believe is the only possible way of carrying out a major repair to a wooden boat at an affordable price. The cost of running a modern boatyard, in labour and taxes, puts many of these institutions out of court for people of modest means who run their boats on a shoe-string. I don't believe that even an efficient yard could have completed the amount of work carried out by David and Ariane inside *Iskra*'s insurance cover, certainly not in the time. Of course we were lucky in several respects. We knew the shipwrights and had every confidence in their skill and the level of their commitment, we had the support of the insurance company. We were lucky to find the shed at Croabh Haven, lucky in the people who worked there and round about, lucky that Adrian happened to be at home when I telephoned him. Without him, I do not believe we would have succeeded. We were lucky in having the help of Richard and Mary and above all, we were lucky to be able to devote our own undivided energies to the job in hand. *Iskra* herself contributed to her own good fortune by a dozen lucky choices and chances that could as easily have gone against her. It must be said that the person coming out of the affair with least credit is myself. I have an excuse which might, or might not hold water. I had been taking a drug for a condition called Paroximal Tachycardia, an affliction I have since mastered by natural means. Wendy believes that this drug slowed down my thinking, gave me a false feeling of complacency that led me to a series of poorly thought out decisions and actions. I hope she's right. After Gigha I stopped taking the drug, for ever I hope.

Apart from any other consideration, *Iskra* would have been destroyed if we had taken her to the Crinan yard. The whole place, boats, gear and all, went up in smoke in the middle of April of 1993. The yard and the chandlery and the stores were burnt down, some of the laid up boats wrecked by fire. *Iskra* had come out of her tussle with the rocks of Gigha stronger and better than when she went into it. She wasn't finished with us yet – she was still to exact two more tolls.

We went to Scotland in the bus again in the Spring of 1993. It was cold, a bitter northerly whistling through the yard where *Iskra* stood. We rented the little house for a week while we made ready for living aboard again. John Macinnes stepped the mast and lifted her gently into the water. She didn't leak a drop. Now when we walked up the lane to Kennels Cottage the rhododendrons made a blazing tunnel of colour for us to pass through. In the morning we heard the piper in the big house breaking the new day for the Dowager Duchess. The Scottish countryside was as beautiful in the spring as it had been in the autumn, the view from the cottage softer now with spring colours, the same suspicion of haunting romance.

Now that the worry and tension of repairing *Iskra* was no longer with us we had time to look around us. We discovered the walk to Ardfern and back along the shores of the loch – it was a tougher walk than we had bargained for, more rewarding than we had imagined. We had to climb over rocks, ford tumbling burns, push through undergrowth, skirt bogs, climb over stone walls. We saw wild deer, wild cats, birds we could not name. We passed through long deserted crofts, their bleak, roofless walls offering a glimpse of a Scotland long since passed. Scotland suffered two devastating convulsions in the 18th and early 19th Centuries – the effects of both still clear to be seen. Bonnie Prince Charlie's ill-planned, ill-generalled and ill-conceived uprising of 1745 led to the bitter and bloody defeat of the Scots at Culloden. The break up of the clan system after Culloden led to the clearances, the end of crofting and mass immigration to Canada, America and Australia. Black Highland cattle and, later, sheep, took the place of people. The English army, aided by many lowland Scots it must be said, embarked on a genocidal spree after Culloden. Anyone remotely connected with the rebellion was hounded down and killed – men, women and children without mercy. Women were left naked outside their burnt houses and crofts to die of cold, their children murdered.

The English soldiers, right up to the Duke of Cumberland, the commander of the King's army, enriched themselves by plundering, from the entire contents of great houses to the cattle, clothing and most meagre possessions of the poor. Many Scottish housewives, not remotely connected with the rebellion, who had billeted English officers in their houses, found themselves and their families stripped of everything down to bed linen and cutlery. It was all sent to England in an endless caravan of wagons. Culloden cowed and dispirited the people of the Highlands with a display of cruelty and avarice not equalled even by Napoleon's soldiers. The wonder of it is that English people like us can still be accepted in Scotland. The clearances completed the depopulation of Scotland with equally ruthless efficiency. In addition they left a scar across this beautiful country that has never healed.

After Culloden the new lairds, with vastly increased land holdings, turned the economy from small croft agriculture to one based on cattle and sheep. The crofters were no longer wanted but their land suddenly increased in value. Big grazing herds on big holdings allowed money to be made on an undreamed of scale. Much wanted meat could be sold to a rapidly increasing English army and population – the crofters had to go. There were thousands and thousands of crofts, each cultivating a small plot of land, supplying food for themselves and for local sale, each family living in the stone houses whose ruins still haunt the countryside. The land was never over farmed, the trees which covered all Scotland, carefully coppiced for controlled felling to supply timber and fuel. But the crofters, inheriting their living from the clan system, were never their own landlords.

As soon as the land became concentrated into big holdings

they found themselves at the mercy of landowners they never knew and had never seen. This was a far cry from the tightly knit clans, where every soul knew his place, his duties, his responsibilities from laird to humblest peasant. These new faceless lairds appointed agents who carried out cruel evictions all over the Highlands and islands. No mercy was shown in the pursuit of profit. In 1831 alone, 58,000 homeless, poverty stricken, bewildered crofters, crushed into the immigrant ships, a year later 66,000. The total was reckoned in millions. Australia, Canada were the gainers in this great migration, Scotland the losers. Scottish communities were founded all over the world that flourish to this day. Scotland is depopulated, its countryside laid waste. It still has its wild beauty, romanticised from Victorian times onwards, but the glory of trees, the settled tranquility of a thriving agriculture are missing.

For a spell the clearances brought prosperity to a decimated population, riches to a tiny few. In the end, sheep destroyed the land. The trees were felled in millions to make way for sheep runs, intensive grazing made sure they never came back. Now Scotland is a shadow of what might have been. Vast tracts of land are given over to the pleasures of shooting for a few brave sportsmen, vast tracts are private, access denied to ordinary people. Japanese, Germans, Frenchmen, anyone with the ready, are buying in. The 'PRIVATE – KEEP OUT' notices (in English) are going up wholesale.

In a week *Iskra* was ready for us to live aboard again, lying snug against the marina pontoon in her new paint, looking for all the world as if nothing had ever been amiss with her. My Dolphin was a smart fellow again, tucked under the new bowsprit, new paint on his new tail, the glint of new promise in his eye, his defection forgiven him, his misdeeds buried in the past. We reckoned Croabh Haven had done us proud. Everyone from top to bottom had gone out of his way to help us. To settle ourselves in, we cruised gently to the north for twenty odd miles to pick up the mooring off Richard and

Mary's house in Connel. It was calm as we pottered across Loch Melford, wormed our way through Cuan Sound and anchored in Puilladobhrain, a pleasant place much favoured by yachts. We walked across to Clachan Sound and the 'bridge over the Atlantic', a gracious stone arch built in 1791 joining Seil Island to the mainland. After Culloden the wearing of the kilt was banned on pain of deportation to the colonies. The clansmen would change from trews to kilts when they came back to the island, where they knew there were no English. The 'Tigh and Truish' pub, which is Gaelic for 'the house of the trews', is hard by the bridge. *Iskra* leaked through her topsides when we first went out in a strong wind but she soon took up. We bought her a new electric pump in Oban and left her for a week on Richard's mooring, which is just outside his house, caught the bus to London to go to a wedding. When we came back she had made no water. We considered that in all respects she had been returned to us.

We sailed the fifty odd miles back to Gigha in calm seas, blue skies, the benign and beautiful seascape which is the west of Scotland in fine summer weather. We sailed into a very different Ardminish Bay. A gentle breeze wafted from the west, warm, welcoming, placid, the Minister's house in bright perspective against the soft, green hills, the ferry ramp with children bathing, the boathouse and Catriona's café, striped umbrellas in the sunshine. One buoy was vacant among a score of yachts. It was the very one we had been on before. This time *Iskra* was shackled to it with two heavy lines made up for the purpose, an iron thimble spliced into one end – the wisdom of hindsight. Every other boat was made fast with a simple bight of rope through the buoy, both ends taken back on board, just as I had made *Iskra* fast on the evening of September 5th. There would be chaos in Ardminish Bay in another sudden easterly gale.

It was something of a triumphant return. We soon found all our friends, we ran into dozens whose names we didn't know. The whole island seemed delighted to see *Iskra* all smart and trim after her brush with the rocks. We went and looked at the rocks themselves, marvelled once again that she could ever have been extricated from such a predicament. We paced out the patch of pure sand she had been on – it was just two feet shorter than her keel. We could still distinguish a scrape on the rock we had forced her over, otherwise there was no sign that she had ever been. Now the purple sea lavender was all over the cove, a pair of seals swam lazily across the entrance, terns dived for fish. *Iskra's* path to open water looked more tortuous, more unlikely than before.

We found John up a ladder repairing the roof of the shop – the island had a new laird and John was employed again. John is a skilled tradesman, carpenter and joiner. Catriona was no longer running her café at the boathouse. She wasn't sure what her future would be under the new laird. Everyone on the island seemed to be waiting with some apprehension, to see which way the new laird would jump. Later, Catriona left he island and her house, leaving behind all the improvements she had made to it. The new laird owns a chain of yacht marinas and camping sites. We heard of plans to turn Gigha into something of a yachting and camping centre. We visited the gardens of Achamore House. They are among the finest in Scotland, famous for rhododendrons and azaleas as well as some rare shrubs. They were planned and planted by Sir James Horlicks in 1949.

Graham was delighted to see *Iskra* back. He and John came on board and examined her with great interest. "She's a fine wee ship," Graham said. We all went to dinner with Vie as an official celebration of *Iskra's* return to health. This time Wendy and I biked all over the island, wandered round the rocky shores and swam from beaches washed by the warm Gulf Stream. We went and saw the Minister and Gudrun, his wife. With great generosity the Minister apologised for his attitude towards me when *Iskra* was wrecked. "I'm sorry," he said, "I thought you were just a stupid yachtsman who ought to know better." Perhaps he was right – I'm still not sure. Later, we were told, the Minister fell foul of the new laird for supporting one of the tenants who was made to leave his house.

We found Iain Wilkieson at the south end of the island, drank coffee with him and relived the saga in the cove, explored the rock-pools round the wreck of the Russian ship. For the first few months she had polluted the island when the wind was north-westerly but now the smell of rotting fish had left her. Archie McAllister's boy, and Catriona's son spent hours on board *Iskra* and looked after our rubber dinghy for us when we were ashore. Margaret and Seamus McSporran gave us a good welcome. Gigha was an experience we will never forget, our return an exercise in nostalgia. In common with all the west of Scotland, Gigha had a much larger population before the clearances. In 1791 it was 614 and it remained at or about that figure until the 20th Century. Now it hovers around the 120 mark.

We left Gigha in a calm but breeze came from the north west before we were out of the Sound. The rocks and the little island of Dearg Sgir and the pleasant beach where we had watched baby seals in play, slid away as *Iskra* settled herself to flog against the freshening wind. It was a fine, brisk sail but rough in the Sound of Jura; we were pleased enough to gain the shelter of Loch Sween. John Macinnes lives in Tayvallich near the top of the loch – a small, enclosed bay with a narrow entrance guarded by a line of rocks. The village straggles round the shore and up the sides of the loch, it would be hard to find a safer, more peaceful haven. We soon found John's house and made ourselves known to Jane and two delightful children.

The Taynish peninsula, a narrow finger some two miles long, runs beside Loch Sween. It is an example of the oak dominated woodland which used to adorn Argyll. The woodland has occupied the peninsula for thousands of years, since trees returned after the last Ice Age. It remains undeveloped, unbuilt on, unspoiled, but well coppiced and carefully looked after by Scottish Natural Heritage. We saw big, bright blue dragonflies, dozens of birds, redstart, woodwarbler, a fleeting glimpse of a roe deer; there are badgers and otters in the forest. We picnicked in a ruined mill, walked all the way to Taynish House where the woodland opens out into a grassy sward, a fine view of Loch Sween and the castle on the other side.

On Monday John and Jane both went off to work, we sailed idly along the steep, wooded shores of the loch to find shelter for the night in a small island called Eilean Mor, helped by a pilot book loaned to us by John. We dropped anchor in the middle of a round bay, not much bigger than a fair sized pond, ran lines to ancient ring bolts let into the rock on either quarter. The island is no more than a mile long, a quarter of a mile across yet between the 8th and the 13th Centuries it supported a colony of monks. It must have been covered with trees and wisely managed. There is a stone chapel built by St Cormic in the 12th Century, partially ruined with only half a roof but beautifully proportioned with three foot thick stone walls and a domed stone roof over the chancel. St Cormic was an ascetic character. Not content with the rigours of life as it was on Eilean Mor he would retire across the island, past the ancient Celtic cross on the brow and down to a tiny chapel, older even than the church, with a cave-like grotto beside it. Here there was hardly room to move but he would stay there, as an additional penance, for days on end. "Uncomfortable," Wendy pronounced it. From the top of the island there is a view over the Sound to the Paps of Jura. Eilean Mor is full of profound religious intensity which neither of us could help being affected by. We have felt it before in simple, lonely places – seldom in great churches and cathedrals.

We cruised up the west coast of Scotland, which is what we had decided to do, it seemed an age ago when we were in Douarnanez. It was as rewarding as we had always expected it to be. It is an understatement to say that the weather is not often good but, of course, we did not expect to find unbroken sunshine. The weather can be treacherous and must be carefully watched but it has its compensations. It keeps Scotland clear of the massed hoards of sun-seeking holidaymakers who can turn a beautiful place into a slum, as they have done in parts of Spain. It brings its own wild beauty with blustery, rain-

His misdeeds forgiven him.

The Russian factory ship.

John, Vie and Graham.

streaked winds coursing through the islands and clothing the
mountains in low cloud, flashes of bright sunshine flooding
colour across the sea and the rocky shore-line. It is a place of
vigour and movement, soaked in a history that is never far
below the surface. It suggests adventure.

We made our way up through the Sound of Mull to
Tobermory, explored the island in a hired car, across to
Fionnphort and over the ferry to Iona. St Columba came
from Ireland to found the monastery in 563 and lived on the
island until he died thirty four years later. It had been a
religious centre since Druid times, St Columba and his
missionaries made it into the Christian centre of Europe. The
book of Kells, now in Dublin, was first started on Iona. In 1500
the monastery was granted Cathedral status. Forty-eight kings
of Scotland, four Irish kings and eight Norwegian were buried
in Iona, including King Duncan, murdered by Macbeth.
Every year half a million visitors come to the island. To us, the
feeling of Godliness was missing; Eilean Mor is a better place
to find God if you are looking for Him.

I have never been to the Outer Hebrides; I have been told
that the islands are a less attractive cruising ground than
mainland Scotland. They are largely bare of trees having been
subjected to the same treatment as the mainland at the time
of the clearances. They are well placed for good, safe
anchorages. The islands have many fervent devotees, John
Macinnes among them, to extol their virtues and to tell of
their romance and fascination. We had intended to sail from
Skye at least to North Uist and Harris but when we got to
Portree the weather began to look nasty. We had a long way
to go round Cape Wrath, across to the Pentland Firth and
down the English coast – we were beginning to think of home.
There were still some lovely places on the mainland, it was
already August. We watched the weather closely and sailed
north with some caution. There can be few lovelier places to
cruise in northern climes than the west of Scotland. Some
years ago I took *Iskra* to Norway and cruised up to the Sonje
Fiord, about half way up the west coast. It was beautiful, but

not in the way Scotland is beautiful. The fiords are higher and deeper and longer and more spectacular than in Scotland but they lack Scotland's intimacy and essential tranquility. I always felt the snow-capped mountains and the sheer size and loneliness of the place were in some way oppressive, even threatening. I felt, in *Iskra*, that we had somehow strayed out of our proper dimension, that we had become small people in a huge world. In Scotland we felt comfortable, a country it would be easy to belong to. We could understand the fierce feeling of pride in their country that Scottish people have.

The Summer Isles are scattered across the entrance to Loch Broom and Little Loch Broom like a child's bricks spread over the nursery floor. We selected a sheltered bay on the island of Tanera Mor as our anchorage for the night. It was a bad choice – we had anchored near a fish farm. Salmon are reared and fattened in captivity all around the west coast. They are a pathetic sight, better not to be seen if you wish to enjoy salmon for supper. Fish farming is comparatively new in Scotland although it is an ancient art. It has been practised in China since at least 2000 B.C. In 475 B.C. Fan Lai wrote a thesis on Carp Culture. The Romans did it on a big scale and in mediaeval times fish were stocked in castle moats and monastery stew ponds. Of a total of 65 or 70 million tons of fish caught over the world every year, fish farming accounts for some 8 million tons, the Chinese still far and away the biggest operators. Nearly a third of the world fish catch is made into fertilizers and fish meal for animal feed. Many of the lochs, right up the west coast of Scotland have salmon farms. They are not a pretty sight.

The salmon is one of nature's more remarkable miracles. It is hatched in fresh water, sometimes far up a river, sometimes above rapids, waterfalls, weirs. The eggs, about a quarter inch in diameter, are laid in a depression on the sandy bottom of a stream which the salmon scoops out with her tail and fins and by pressing into the sand with her body. The eggs are fertilized by her partner at the same time. She covers the eggs with fine sand and leaves them to incubate. She is in bad shape by this time, having eaten nothing since coming in to fresh water and she makes her way back to the sea, leaving the eggs to get on with it by themselves. In four or five months the babies, about three-quarters of an inch long, are hatched. They are quite helpless and live hidden under a stone on the bed of the stream, feeding from the yolk sac they are born with.

When the tiny fish get bigger, about 1½ inches long, they start swimming about looking for food. They stay in the river until they are two years old, sometimes longer and then they set off for the sea, young fish about 6 or 8 inches long. Once at sea they stay around the estuary for a spell, turning a pale pink in colour, growing ever bigger and stronger. Then the young salmon goes out into the ocean. He goes off on journeys measured in thousands of miles. Sometimes he spends four or five years in the ocean before he comes back to spawn, the longer he stays, the bigger he becomes – the biggest salmon ever landed in England weighed 83lbs. To spawn, the salmon makes his way over all those miles of ocean, back to the same estuary, up the same river, leaping rapids, jumping over steep waterfalls. Salmon can jump vertically, three times their own length. Finally they nose their way back, often to the very spot where they were hatched themselves, to deposit another clutch of eggs.

Human beings, of course, know how to do these things more efficiently and cost effectively. There's no more leaving it to the hit or miss of nature. The salmon are grown in hatcheries scattered up and down the lochs of Scotland. When they grow to maturity they are crowded in their thousands into floating wire and net cages moored by the side of the loch. They are artificially fed, kept free of disease by the application of a range of pesticides. There was a seven-fold expansion of fish farming in Scotland between 1985 and 1990, in 1989 there were 337 salmon farms in the west of Scotland. Numbers may have declined since the bandwagon began to slow down. The industry has been allowed to develop without national guidelines and is virtually free of controls.

Dangerous chemicals are used and a high level of pollution caused with few strict controls imposed. A highly dangerous chemical called Dichlorvos has been widely used to treat sea lice, a common parasite in intensive fish farming. This chemical is deadly to shellfish – and to human beings.

Because the fish never see the ocean, their flesh never attains the pink, salmon colour that is a commercial imperative. They are given another dangerous chemical, Canthaxanthin, to make them pink. There is a popular myth that fish feel no pain and therefore suffer no discomfort. In fact, they are vertebrates and have a brain, spinal chord and nerves. They are sensitive to light, dark, smell, taste, noise and stress but they are exempt from the legal protection enjoyed by other animals. Sometimes at slaughter they are frozen alive to die by slow suffocation, sometimes their gills are slit and they are left to bleed to death in the water, sometimes they are electrocuted or, more humanely, stunned with a club.

Waste products from intensive feeding and from the various chemicals used, fall to the bottom under the cages and combine with the fish droppings to pollute the bottom of the loch, forming a kind of emulsion which kills plants, poisons shellfish. Sometimes a poisonous algae is formed under the cages. Rent is charged by the Crown Estates which owns the seabed in the lochs. A lease for a five hundred ton farm will bring the Crown Estates £25,000 per year. Their primary interest is to make profits, their concern for the environment, or for the salmon, is marginal. The monitoring and inspection procedures for the industry are quite inadequate.

Fish farming is clearly with us to stay, regardless of ethics. There is another way of farming salmon, known as ranching, which avoids the worst cruelties and many of the diseases. The young fish are allowed their freedom. They go off, like their natural cousins, their homing instinct bringing them back to the salmon farm as mature fish to spawn and then be fattened for the market.

To be a permanent source of prosperity to the west of Scotland, without a major destruction of the environment, the industry should be properly controlled by an independent authority, properly managed and maintained. The cage we had anchored beside was packed tight with mature fish – there were hundreds, perhaps thousands of them. We watched as they leapt vainly in the air, turning and twisting as if to discover a way to freedom, to the life their instinct told them nature had intended them for. The smell of the place and the sound of these lovely creatures churning up the putrid water of their prison drove us away to a more salubrious spot.

By now the weather was mostly grey with only occasional fleeting patches of sunlight, sometimes threatening. We sailed up through the Minch to Loch Inchard, across the beautiful bay of Endrachillis, a place of small islands, a view of the far Hebrides against an angry sunset. The midget submarines that mined the *Tirpitz* in 1943 in a Norwegian fiord were trained and based in Endrachillis Bay. The last haven before Cape Wrath is Kinlochbervie where we waited for reasonable weather, probably the busiest fishing port in the west of Scotland. The fishermen helped us to a quiet corner of the harbour alongside a wooden pontoon well out of the way. On Friday the whole fleet comes in, filling every inch of every space, packed boat alongside boat across the harbour. The fish market, in a great warehouse all along one side of the jetty, was a huge operation with hundreds of dealers bidding for the week's catch, tons of fish changing hands, large sums of money bandied about. With some trepidation we asked for some haddock for our supper. We were given enough to keep us for a week – fish, fish soup, fish pie and fish stew. They would accept no money. "Ye can put a pound in the Mission box."

The Mission to Deep Sea Fishermen is to be found in a dozen Scottish harbours. Sailors can sleep, or get a meal or buy cheap clothing or pass the time of day with a cup of coffee. They are friendly places, always welcoming to anyone coming from the sea, run by devoted volunteer ladies. We always found we could meet someone in the Mission who would know about tides or moorings or the best place to lie in a harbour. When the market was over, the fish all moved out in refrigerated trucks, the fishermen all went home for a couple of days and Kinlochbervie was deserted. Most of them live on the east coast. We made a proper stow, filled our tanks with cheap fishermen's diesel, bought our stores at the little shop and waited for a break in the strong north west winds. "I'm afraid it will be a rough passage but we might be here for weeks if we wait for fine weather," I warned Wendy. "Let's get on," she said, "it will be better on the east coast."

The wind showed no inclination to ease but after a couple of days it was forecast to back to the south-west which would at least give us a slant once we cleared the breaking rock four miles off the entrance to Loch Inchard. It was forecast to increase but I reckoned if we left early, we would get through the overfalls off the cape at slack water and once round, the wind would be from the land. I tucked the reefs into the mains'l, bent on a small jib and we left at five in the morning. As soon as we came out of the shelter in Kinlochbervie and into Loch Inchard we realised that it was blowing harder than we had imagined. I wondered out loud whether we ought to go on or turn back, "Let's go on," Wendy repeated – "if it's safe." It had backed to west-south-west, was gusting up to Force 7.

With everything trim and the sheets hardened we could just point a course to bring us clear of Roin Beag at the entrance to the loch. "Once we get clear we can ease the sheets and it will be better." As we passed through the narrow entrance to the loch *Iskra* came free of shelter, bursting into a maelstrom of wind and sea. She shuddered, shook herself, put her lee rail under and hurled herself forward. A big sea broke over the bow, rolled across the cabin top, sending spray half way up the mast. Another she hit straight on, bringing herself up short. Then she seemed to find a way of clawing herself slowly ahead.

Soon the seas across the entrance lengthened and slowly smoothed themselves. The rocks to leeward were moving past but now she was hardly pointing the course. Perhaps a bit of current was setting her to leeward. Roin Beag was dead under the bowsprit, still about a mile to go. "She needs the stays'l." I got myself for'ard, unclipped the halyard from the shrouds. I should have hoisted the stays'l before – now it was near impossible. The foredeck was dipping deep under, as she came up she brought half a ton of water with her that cascaded overboard with great force. Kneeling on the deck, holding hard to the lifeline, I was hardly strong enough to hang on. "Leave it," Wendy shouted from aft, "leave it till later." I came back to the cockpit, left the halyard clipped to the stay, glanced at the rock, closer now and still on the bowsprit. We were not weathering it. "I can't leave it – if we have to go about she may miss stays without the stays'l – we'll be on the rocks." I tried again. This time I saw a gap in the seas, made a lunge for the bitts, caught the forestay, clipped the halyard to the sail and got back before the next sea broke. I hauled up the halyard, Wendy hardened in the stays'l sheet and at once *Iskra* picked up speed, headed up half a point – just enough to clear the rock. We watched it slide past to leeward a biscuit throw away. A flush of relief went through us, we eased the sheet and *Iskra* raced away to the north on a broad reach.

The ten miles of coast between Loch Inchard and Cape Wrath is a bleak, wild place. Soon we could see the black cliffs of the cape, the coastline gradually steepening and becoming more rugged as it goes north. At first there is a bay called Sandwood with a bright beach of pure, untrodden sand. There is no road to Sandwood Bay, only a tortuous track. In the days before the lighthouse on Cape Wrath was built it was a notorious place for shipwrecks – their bones can still be seen against the sand. A mermaid, often seen by shepherds, lives on Am Balg, a rock a mile off the sand. She it was who persuaded mariners that Am Balg was Duslic Rock, a mile north of the cape, so that they thought they were in safe waters if they passed to seaward of it. The Bay is still said to have some spiritual blight on it, giving off an indefinable feeling of unease and dread. This has been believed for centuries. We were having our breakfast by the time we passed Am Balg; I kept a close look out but saw no mermaid.

The wind freshened steadily as we came up with the cape. *Iskra* was hard to hold on a dead run but I hung on to the mains'l – we would be in a good lee once we were round. It was slack water. We passed the cape no more than half a mile off, inside Duslic Rock, surged through the confused, lumpy seas and gybed round in what would become dangerous overfalls when the tide started to run. The black cliffs towered above us, a giant slab of rock reared up beside the lighthouse, perched above like some heavenly eye. Razorbills, kittiwakes, guillemots and the chubby puffins wheeled and dived and screamed their outrage at our intrusion into their world. We found smoother seas as we brought the wind on our quarter and felt the lee of the cliffs, sailed in safety and at our ease past one of the most awe-inspiring coastlines to be found in Britain – wild, desolate, lonely, beautiful in its brutality.

As was often the case it was the women of Durness who offered the fiercest resistance to the landlords' sheriffs at the time of the clearances. In Durness the sheriff timed his call, as was his habit, so that the men were working on their crofts, the women and children at home. But he met a militant brand of housewives. They seized the sheriff by the hand that held the official eviction papers, held it over the fire until he dropped them into the flames, so the story has it. In fact there was a real battle between crofters and the law in Durness, but it didn't end happily for the crofters. The superintendent of police came to remonstrate with the crofters but he too was driven off. Next he came with a posse of constables. They were routed by the local people armed with clubs. Then the law came back in force and the 53rd Regiment in Edinburgh was put on alert. Now the men were home from fishing and from the fields and they joined forces with their militant wives, armed with stones they carried in their aprons. There were 300 people on the cliff road in a highly excited state, screaming vengeance on all who tried to lay hands on their homes. There was a serious fight. The law managed to gain entrance to the inn for the night where they barred and shuttered themselves in but at 10 o'clock the people assaulted the inn, broke down the door and after a furious battle dragged the constables out. Having chased the constables into the hills they found the sheriff and the Procurator Fiscal who, with some courage, had stood their ground. Some wanted to "strip them naked and turn them out on the rocks" but eventually they were allowed to leave in their horse and gig for the nearest inn, some 20 miles distant, where they arrived at 5 in the morning. A few days later, resistance collapsed like a burst bubble. The Sheriff of Sutherland came to Durness with a collection of worthies and officials and the threat of immediate orders to the 53rd Regiment to move in. The people changed from tigers to mice, the Minister (always on the side of the law) persuaded them to write a letter of apology. They promised to leave their lands and homes peacefully. In six months they were packed like cattle into the immigrant ships and the land was given over to sheep. This extraordinary submissiveness, seen throughout the history of the clearances, must have stemmed from that cataclysmic defeat at Culloden and the terrible retribution that was exacted on the highlands.

The wind eased and the day fined and the sea smoothed itself and Wendy came out of her usual mini coma of seasickness as we sailed across the north of Scotland. We passed the implicit threat of the nuclear power station at Dounreay, with its gleaming sphere, without mishap, rounded Holborn Head and were tied alongside at Scrabster for supper. We found another Mission for Deep Sea Fishermen, another group of friendly people. We had damaged the gaff jaws in an accidental gybe on the west coast – they were repaired by a friend of a friend in a little workshop near the quay. Once more we were given precise instructions for passing safely through Pentland. "Go through the Inner Sound inside Stroma – keep well in and ye'll miss the overfalls." They were right. It was rough off Dunnet Head, the wind had freshened again, but still a fair wind from the west.   Once past the Head we kept inshore as instructed, skirted inside the worst of the overfall and sailed through in great comfort close past the tall rock columns of Duncansby Head. Soon we were on the east coast again, pointing straight for home. Wendy had been dreaming about the terrors of the Pentland Firth – she heaved a sigh of relief as we rounded the massive and noble headland, a brisk north-west wind took us at a fast clip to Wick.

11

Last Squall

The east coast is much neglected by the cruising fraternity although it offers many pleasant surprises and has, in places, a spectacular coastline. It can be an unpleasant coast in a hard easterly wind but in the summer, when westerlies are, or at least used to be the norm, it is a delight. Wick has much to commend it as a place to be gale bound in. We used the southerly direction of the gale, which sprang up soon after we reached Wick, to ride our bicycles up to Duncansby Head, an even more spectacular bastion from the land than from the sea. Deep fissures in the rock face give glimpses of the breaking water far below, millions of sea-birds nesting precariously against the sheer rock face. We observed the Pentland Firth in a gale from the comfort of the cliff top and were thankful we had sneaked through in calm weather.

As we watched the sea from the east side of the Cape we saw a group of hundreds of seals all congregated together in a tight group below us within 20 yards of the shore, for all the world as if they were attending some conference, or political or religious meeting. Perhaps they were. There was a kind of hum of low growls and mumbles and an occasional roar. Then, to our astonishment as we watched, they all up-ended their bottoms and dived together so that every one of them disappeared simultaneously from our view. There must have been some reason, some master seal in charge of the operation or perhaps an instinctive group impulse. We watched for five minutes and then, as suddenly, they all broke surface again and continued with their discussion. We could think of no explanation for this eccentric behaviour. We folded our bicycles into their bags and thumbed a lift back to Wick against the wind, with a group of travelling actors. They go to remote schools and villages in the Highlands with their children's theatre.

Wick is an early example of enlightened town planning. The newer part of the town on the west side of the river and the harbour was designed by Thomas Telford at the beginning of the 19th Century. It was built by the British Fisheries Society, set up by Act of Parliament to give evicted crofters new employment in the fishing industry. It was at the beginning of the herring boom that lasted for a hundred years and brought employment and some prosperity to the east coast. When the new town was built at least one group of 1,500 young men and women walked the 130 miles across the north of Scotland from the west of Sutherland to find work in Wick. It took them seven days, they found no shelter on the journey, slept in the open. Wick no longer has much of a fishing industry but it still has the spacious, dignified atmosphere Telford gave it.

We left Wick early in the morning in a strong north-west wind which was forecast to increase to a gale, but there was no real danger in it. We didn't want to miss the chance of a fair wind. With storm trys'l and stays'l, the wind on the quarter, *Iskra* was perfectly contained within herself and had no difficulty with the rough seas in the Moray Firth. Fraserburgh has a good radio beacon, simplifying our landfall. We covered the sixty odd miles in ten hours, arriving in Fraserburgh at tea time to find half a dozen Dutch and French yachts sheltering from the gale. Our only regret was that we had not spent time in the small fishing ports and harbours along the south shore of the Firth.

We started the engine and clawed down the sails as the gale swept us round the harbour mole. With no more than a quarter of a mile to reach the quay we had the gale and the current ahead – our engine, flat out, could only just breast the tide and the wind. By hugging the harbour wall we found a brief lee and made a few yards of headway. By luck we managed to pass a line to the last yacht on the trot and he hauled us alongside.

The engine was hot. I reached in to stop it and saw that the pressure had dropped to zero. It had lost its oil – I could think of no reason for it. The owner of the next boat was a fat Dutchman in a very smart new yacht. "I'll look at it for you," he volunteered, "I'm a ship's engineer – I know about small diesel engines." I stripped the covers off and he came on board, immaculate in a white boiler suit. "Where did you get this?" he demanded as soon as he saw the engine. "It is as old as I am." "Possibly," I said, "but it's in good shape." "Good shape? It's a wreck – it would make a good mooring." He heaped scorn on *Iskra*'s noble old engine as he prodded it, tapped it, listened to it and looked round it to the limit of dirtying his boiler suit. "The sump is cracked, the piston is burnt out. The best thing you can do is to throw it out," were his parting remarks.

We were in a state of gloom as we went for our evening walk. "We'll stay another day," I said, "that Dutchman's going in the morning – I'll have another look at the engine." When he had gone I stripped the covers off again, started the old engine. It sounded as sweet as ever. I crawled in beside it, forced my head down into the bilge from where I could see the sump. No leak. As I twisted round to extricate myself my eye caught the bottom of the hand pump for the sump oil. It was dripping oil. Wendy increased the revs and it came out in a steady stream. Covered in oil but triumphant I stripped the pump, found a blocked valve, cleared it. The leak stopped.

"All the same," Wendy said, "he was right – we do need a new engine."

"Nonsense," I snapped.

As we progressed down our familiar east coast the engine threw another temperament. It began to leak oil through the seal in the main bearing so that the drips were spread all around by the flywheel. It was a disease the engine had once before and I knew how to cure it. We lived with it all down the coast, using the engine as little as possible, sailing up the Tay Estuary and into Dundee, into the tiny harbour close under St Abbs Head, into Eyemouth and the walled city of Berwick-on-

Tweed. We had a fine day and a hard north-west wind to sail past the Farne Islands and the lovely Northumberland coast to Amble. We sailed close past mediaeval castles, mile on mile of deserted beach and gracious mansions set in woods and rolling countryside. We called at Blyth and then Hartlepool on the south side of the Tyne. Soon we were in Whitby for another look at the museum and Captain Cook's house, then across the Wash to Lowestoft – spitting distance from home.

Our voyage had started innocently enough, the simple proposition of a visit to the caves of Altamira. It had assumed a wayward course, taking us where we had never intended to go and involving us in experiences we would have wished to avoid. It was as if *Iskra* had taken charge of the whole operation and used the voyage to further her own ends. In this, it could not be denied, she had succeeded. She was a better, stronger, sounder boat at the end than she had been at the beginning. If she had been forced to wring out of us the care she ought to have had by right of her great age and her nobility, so be it. She clearly considers herself justified in getting what she needs by whatever means she can find. As her carers, this is a cross we are content to bear. At least she is in the habit of throwing her temperaments in circumstances and in situations where the possibility of redress for her grievance is at least feasible. She might have wrecked herself on any one of dozens of places she has been where help for her or for us was out of the question. In Lowestoft, the voyage was almost but not quite finished. She still had two items on her list which were not yet ticked off. Since so much had been done for her, she may have surmised, we might as well go the whole hog and give her everything she needed.

Lowestoft is a place we like, where *Iskra* is known and where we have friends; just the place to repair the oil leak in the engine which was beginning to make life a misery. It was only a drip of oil but the flywheel distributed it around, coating everything within its radius with a film of oil. We motored through the swing bridge and for a mile across Lake Lothing to a berth in the Cruising Club. By the time we got there we were ready to make a mooring of the engine. A friend at the Club told us about another member who ran a small yard in Lowestoft and who was a good engineer. We rode our bikes back along a part of the Lowestoft dock system and found Mick Slack in the yard beside the dry dock. He agreed to help us, came on board to look. "It's a noble beast," he said when he saw the engine.

By luck I still had on board the massive extractor tool which we had made in Rio de Janeiro the last time the seal had failed. On that occasion, the new seal we put in was made from a piece of shoe leather because it was all that we could get. Clearly it had been second class stuff. This time, Mick put in a new, rubber seal and the job was properly done. Mick patted the engine on the head as it gently ticked over. "Runs like a charm," he said, "Pity it's not right for the boat – it's slow revving, needs a big prop which you haven't got room for." His partner, David Saunders, is a shipwright, trained in the same school where David had been a teacher. He knew David well, was interested to see *Iskra*'s repair and inspected the work minutely. "This would be a good place to get work done if we need it again," Wendy remarked.

It was a warm, calm, thundery morning when we set off for Bradwell. We motored out of Lowestoft Harbour, the engine running nicely again. "There," I said, "the old engine's fine again – it'll last for years yet." Soon the wind picked up to Force 4. It had been blowing hard the previous day, it was still squally and generally overcast with occasional glimpses of the sun. Not the finest day but it would do. If it turned nasty we could always go in to Southwold – I didn't bother to reef the mains'l. We were relaxed, the voyage was over, the last chapter acted out. Now we were in home waters, no more than a good day's sail from our mooring in Bradwell Creek. We sat with our coffee in the cockpit, the wind off the shore, everything set except the tops'l, the big stays'l pulling *Iskra* along steadily and easily.

Wendy was pleased to be back, so was I. She would busy herself in her much neglected garden, I would attend to a hundred things that had piled up and were crying out for action. We would go off for a few pleasant excursions in what was left of the summer, deliver *Iskra* up to the care of the yard in Maldon for the winter. We reflected on what had befallen us and on our good fortune – disaster turned to profit. A round cloud came up over the land to windward, the muted sound of thunder rumbled around. The wind freshened, *Iskra* took the strain and began to move fast towards home. "Just what we wanted," I said, "if this keeps up we'll go straight on round Orford Ness, before the tide turns." The wind kept up for half an hour. *Iskra* was charging across a flat sea, the water curling away from her bow, hissing through the lee scuppers. Then it eased, the strain came off and she settled to a more modest pace. "Quite a squall," I said, "just as well I hadn't set the tops'l."

Twenty minutes later another round, dark cloud came over the land and the rumblings of thunder increased. We were well on our way towards Orford Ness now, we could clearly see the town of Southwold over to starboard, a pretty town from the sea – lighthouse, church towers, a line of cliff backed by green sward, the twin piers marking the harbour entrance beyond. This squall was not quite as strong as the one before. "Looks like they're taking off a bit – it must be time for coffee."

As the second squall passed over, Wendy put on the kettle, stood in the hatch waiting for it to boil. The next cloud had a little wisp of black hanging down from it, like a stringy black beard. There was more thunder and the wind freshened again, *Iskra* picked up speed again. I was steering on the lee side of the cockpit, watching the luff of the stays'l as it strained against the sheet. It began to rain, the squall freshened again. Wendy passed me my oilskins and I struggled into them in the cockpit. There was lightning followed immediately by claps of thunder, very close.

At first the rain was no more than heavy but suddenly, in another clap of thunder, it became a torrent, then more than a torrent, a solid deluge as if some monster hand had

It was rough in the Moray Firth.

Homeward-bound smiles.

Bald headed without the top of the mast.

A neat scarf.

In with the new.

Out with the old.

Ready for another voyage.

Winter quarters.

upturned a vast bucket to windward of us. It was being blown horizontally across the sea to us, almost a wave of water. *Iskra* staggered. I remember being thankful I had the working jib on her in place of the much bigger sail. Now the wind was fierce, the sun blotted out, a noise like a train in a tunnel. I shouted to Wendy, "I must get the stays'l in – it'll blow out." I watched the straining clew for a moment longer, clipped my harness to the lifeline, notched the tiller into the steering vane. It was heavy – too heavy for Wendy to hold.

Then the squall freshened again, *Iskra* lay right over, the water tearing past half way up the side decks, the rain like a waterfall but driven into our faces so that we could hardly see. It was freezing cold. Next there was an explosion of thunder right on top of us, a report like the firing of a powerful pistol – simultaneously with it a flash of blinding light. Wendy was standing in the hatch facing aft, I was looking up the lee side at the luff of the stays'l, striving to keep her full and bye, knowing the stays'l would blow out if it flapped. As I watched, the mains'l came tumbling down the mast, heaping itself on the coachroof and in the lee scuppers. I looked aloft in time to see the top part of the mast, from the hounds to the truck, descending almost gracefully to the deck. It laid itself gently on top of the bundles of sail, then toppled into the sea to leeward. "We've been struck," Wendy said.

The wind increased again, the rain driven so hard that I couldn't move out of the cockpit, *Iskra* pressed over by the stays'l, still rushing through the flat sea dragging along a flotsam of sails, spars, wires, ropes. The mast was gone from the hounds up, leaving the lower shrouds and the runners and the inner forestay intact, the stays'l still pulling like a shire horse. "I must get it down" – as I said the words the stays'l blew out. It was gone in seconds and seemed to dissolve. I had a fleeting glimpse of the centre part of the sail billowing away across the sea and then all that was left were a few rags up the forestay and a handkerchief of clew, still attached to the sheet. *Iskra* came up, lay quiet, the drooping boom still held by its topping lift, the jib in the sea beside her.

Wendy said, "Are you all right?"

"Yes – how about you?"

"I'm all right – a bit alarmed. The kettle's boiling."

The squall died as soon as it had come, the rain petered out, the wind settled itself in a south-westerly direction as before but now only a light breeze. The little cloud with its black whisker had merged itself into a darkening sky. The sun broke through for a minute. We drank our coffee, surveyed the chaos. "Apart from the mast and the cross trees, I can't see that anything is broken or damaged." We hauled the boom onto the gallows, gathered in the sail and left it half in the scuppers, half tied to the boom and the gaff. It wasn't torn. We hauled the top of the mast on board and wedged it along the lee side. The VHF aerial was undamaged, even the tricolor light at the truck was intact. We hauled the jib on board, cleared away the tangle of ropes and wire and fastened it all down. The cross trees were on the foredeck in two halves.

When everything was clear I started the engine, headed for Southwold no more than two or three miles off. I hauled down the luff of the torn sail, cleared it off the forestay, bent on the working stays'l and sheeted it home. She would just fetch the piers with the engine at full throttle and the stays'l pulling bravely. Mick had made a good job of the engine – there was no oil leak. As we made our way towards Southwold the inshore lifeboat came speeding towards us. She stopped a few yards off on our starboard side, observed us with evident interest for a few minutes. I gave them what I hoped was a confident, carefree wave and they went on their way. She had been called out, we heard, by a yacht off shore with a rope round her propeller.

It was just after half flood. The tide runs strongly in Southwold harbour, a good four knots. The sky was dark again as we approached the harbour entrance. I handed the stays'l, stuffed it through the hatch into the fo'c'sle. We set *Iskra* between the piers, the wind freshening from ahead but the tide under her taking her steadily through the narrow entrance. Then another squall hit us, the wind came shrieking at us from ahead – not as strong this time and without the rain but hard enough to bring *Iskra* to a halt, even with the strong current behind her. I put her in the wind's eye, the engine at full throttle, watched the piers a few yards off on either side as they slid slowly backwards.

It freshened again, suddenly shifting half a point to the north. I put the tiller hard over to bring her head into it but the wind caught the turn of her bow and swung her round towards the port hand pier. "My God – we're going to hit it." I slammed the engine into reverse but nothing would stop her – the bowsprit was making straight for the wood piling. It would go between two piles, would foul itself. As she swung round the bowsprit would break, or worse, it would wrench open the stem. My imagination raced. I saw the whole business of another wreck unfolding before my eyes. I glanced at Wendy – saw that the same macabre picture was flashing through her mind. But *Iskra* was following a different agenda.

She hit the pier but the bowsprit didn't go between the piles. By a chance in a hundred it hit one of the old pilings which was a bit soft and cushioned the blow. Six inches either way it would have slipped between and snarled up. At the same time the engine at last bit in reverse and helped by the flood tide streaming through the pier she came clear as the wind took her bow off. I swung the tiller hard over the other way, put her ahead, she slid down beside the pier, her starboard side inches away from it and then she picked up steerage way and we motored out to sea again against the tide but with the wind behind us. In ten minutes the squall had died and the sky cleared. We waited for a while and then motored in, the flood tide still under us.

The harbour master had been told of our predicament on VHF by the lifeboat and was ready to help us alongside. When we looked closely at the stump of the broken mast we saw that there was a small flaw in it. Someone in the distant past, long before I owned *Iskra*, had fastened the cross trees with two long screws into the mast. I remember dimly taking them out, leaving the cross trees supported by an iron hoop round the mast so that they are free to move laterally. There was a little bit of rot in both the old screw holes.

At first there was doubt in my mind as to whether we had really been struck by lightning. It was almost as if the mast had been cut with a saw, horizontally across just above the hounds. There was no sign of a burn or a scorch mark as might be expected from a lightning strike. On the other hand the stays to the top of the mast were still intact, the navigation light was intact and working. Afterwards, we were told by an expert that it almost certainly was a strike. Because it was raining with great intensity and the whole boat covered with water the current would have been conveyed to earth without doing damage, except in a place where it found a weakness.

There is a good boat yard in Southwold but they were busy and were unwilling to give me a price or to tell me how long the job would take. I telephoned David in Lowestoft. "I'll come this afternoon and look at it," he said. We had squared up most of the mess by the time he and Mick arrived. They looked at the job, gave us a price and told us it would take a week. We sailed her back to Lowestoft on Saturday morning, making slow but steady time with the engine, the working stays'l and the storm trys'l which I was able to set on one of the topping lifts. *Iskra* was an odd sight with her stump and her jury rig. David made a neat, strong scarf in the mast – when it was done it was hard to see the join, he made us a new pair of cross trees to the same high standard.

Our stay in Lowestoft elongated itself. One day while we were in the shed varnishing the newly repaired mast, Mick said to me, "I know you love that engine but one day it will be the end of you – it's very old and it's not powerful enough for the boat. Put it in to honourable retirement and have a new one."

I said, "Never – I wouldn't dream of it – it's good and faithful."

Wendy said, "Do you mean we could have an engine that would go against the tide? One that would go backwards? One that would stop us? One we could get into a marina with?" I was scandalized, resistant. They worked on me, wearing down my resolve, eroding my loyalty, weakening my commitment to an old friend. Always when I had compared my love and my spasmodic hate for it, love had triumphed. Now it was to be betrayed.

Mick was agent for Lombardini, he would let me have the whole installation at a reasonable price. It would be smooth and quiet and powerful and economical. It was a beauty – a four cylinder diesel of 47 horse power against the old engine's 20. Mick said he would restore the old engine, he would use it in the shed as a spare generator in case of a power cut, he would paint it green, he would love it, it would be venerated. My resistance cracked, then crumbled, then evaporated. At the same time David would put in new tanks to replace those that had been damaged in Gigha and while he had the tanks out he would double any cracked timbers under the quarters. They had probably never been looked at since she was built. It was all agreed. When the mast was finished we brought *Iskra* back down through Lake Lothing to the yard, she was craned up on to the dock and wheeled to an open space beside Mick and David's shed. Wendy hired us a caravan by the sea in Lowestoft so that we could commute to the yard every day on our bicycles.

The whole of the cockpit and the bridge deck had to be dismantled to get the old engine out. Whoever had put it in must have built the boat round it. My old companion and friend rose like a phoenix, high in the air on Mick's crane, was laid gently to rest to await its metamorphosis. We cleaned buckets of oily emulsion from where it had lived for so long, scraped the grime off the timbers and painted the bilge. Shiny, new stainless water tanks were put in, the new engine took up its position, settled itself in. David rebuilt the cockpit and the bridge deck leaving us some useful extra space. It was hard to believe that this small, clean, neat looking machine wielded more than twice the clout of our old engine. Mick had the pitch of the old propeller broadened, connected an ingenious network of wires and pipes and gauges and flashing lights, explained to me in great detail the inner workings of the system.

In two weeks we were launched for engine trials up and down Lake Lothing. I had to admit that *Iskra* was transformed – Wendy and I looked at each other in disbelief. In place of the big old iron pipe that had served me as a gear lever for 25 years and the big bronze throttle control connected to the engine through a chain of rods and levers and springs, a small knob gave access to undreamed of power. The merest touch would send *Iskra* leaping ahead at her maximum hull speed, another slight depression would bring her up standing, send her careering astern. This was a new experience for us. We had seen modern boats handled in this way but had never imagined it could happen to us. We took her away from Lowestoft, showed her off in the Suffolk and Essex rivers for a couple of weeks and then, at last, sailed back to Bradwell.

We came into Bradwell in the evening, at the top of the flood tide, round the dog-leg into the creek, past the quay where barges used to lie, past the entrance to the new yacht marina and through the line of moored boats to our own buoy off Pewit Island. It was there, waiting for us. We have been coming back to Bradwell for half a lifetime, it has changed but it has never lost its charm and the profound pleasure of coming home has never left us.

A voyage in a yacht, any voyage long or short, is an entity in itself. We are full of hope and expectation when we set off, full of plans, eager for the new experience every voyage brings. It has a beginning, a middle and an end – there is no certainty about it. We know, or we believe we know where we are going and we believe we know when we will return; other than this loose framework the voyage is wide open to the vagaries of wind and weather and pure chance. Some voyages start well and end badly, a few pursue an even course, every move exactly fitting the predicted plan – others start badly and end well. At the end of it all is Bradwell and home, the ultimate symbol of stability that makes it all possible. The most intrepid travellers are those who are the staunchest lovers of home.

Without home it is impossible to go away, impossible to come back. Whatever the outcome and whatever the afflictions or oppressions that befall us on the way, the voyage when it is all over and done with, notches itself into our memories and stays there for as long as we are able to remember.

As we rowed ashore, the dinghy heavy with our gear, we took a last look at *Iskra*, peacefully at rest for a spell. She looked much as she has always looked, bearing no scar, carrying no mark to tell of her adventures – perhaps a little smug having extracted from us everything she wanted.

We dropped in for a pint at the Green Man, much the same as it has been since I have known it. "Had a good voyage?" the landlord asked us as he passed us our beer. We thought for a moment. "Yes," we said, "a good voyage."

Nautical terms used in the text

Amidships	The middle part of the vessel
Antifouling paint	Specially prepared paint to discourage underwater marine growth
Ballast	Bars of iron or lead placed in the bilge to keep the boat down in the water
Bilge	The bottom of a boat under the cabin sole
Bitts	Stout upright timbers to hold the inner end of the bowsprit. Also used to make fast the anchor chain or mooring ropes.
Block	A pulley, usually made of wood
Boom	Spar along the bottom of the mains'l
Boom gallows	Wooden structure the boom rests on when the mains'l is furled
Bowsprit	Spar protruding over the bow from which a jib can be set
Bulkhead	A partition between two compartments
Bulldog grips	Used for clamping together two parts of wire
Bunk board	A wooden or canvas board to stop the occupant falling out of his bunk
Burgee	Small flag flown from the masthead
Cabin sole	The floor or deck in the cabin
Caravelle	A type of ancient ship
Careen	To pull a boat over on her side by bowsing down on the mast
Caulking cotton	Used for caulking (filling) seams in the hull
Chain plate	Iron straps bolted to the topsides to which shrouds are attached
Cleat	Used for fastening sheets or other ropes
Coach roof	The top of the cabin, raised to give increased headroom
Cockpit	The well at the stern where the helmsman sits
Covering board	The outermost deck plank
Cross trees	Wooden spreaders to separate the shrouds and increase their effectiveness
Cutter	A sailing vessel having one mast and two heads'ls
Dead reckoning	Charting the position without the aid of bearings or sights

158

Draft	The depth of water needed to float a vessel
Eyes of the ship	Close up to the bow either on deck or below
Foc's'le	The for'ard part of a yacht or ship
Forefoot	Heavy timber joining stem and keel
Forestay	Wire, from the hounds to the bow, supporting the mast
Four fold purchase	A tackle with two double blocks
Full and bye	Sailing close hauled with the sails well filled
Gaff	Spar holding the head of the mains'l
Gaff cutter	A cutter having a 4-sided as opposed to a triangular mains'l
Gaff jaws	Leathered saddle to allow the gaff to slide on the mast
Grapnel	Small anchor with several flukes
Gybe	When the boom swings over as the wind crosses the stern
Handy billy	A small tackle having a single and a double block
Heave-to	To take the way off a vessel by backing the sails
Helm	Another word for tiller
Hemp	A natural fibre rope or twine
Hounds	Where the main shrouds and the cross trees are fastened, towards the top of the mast
Jib	The for'ard of two heads'ls carried by a cutter
Jury rig	An improvised rig used in an emergency
Keelson	Internal timber bolted to the top of the keel
Lee	The lee, or lee'ard side is the down wind side
Mains'l	The sail set on the after side of the mast. Usually the biggest sail
Marlin	Fibre line used for seizing (binding) and many other purposes
Mayday	A distress call - only used in extreme emergency
Pan Pan	A distress call - less urgent than Mayday
Peak halyard	Used to hoist and lower the end of the gaff
Pinnace	A ship's boat, propelled with oars
Pintle	Support for the rudder which allows it to turn freely
Port	The left hand side
Reef	To reef is to shorten sail
Rigging screws	Turnbuckles used to tension the shrouds

Runners	Wire stays from the mast to the deck, supporting the mast
Scandalise	To reduce sail by lowering the peak
Scuppers	Drains for water to run away off the deck
Seacock	Valve in the hull to let in sea water
Sheets	The ropes controlling the sails
Shrouds	Wires supporting the mast
Sights	A sextant reading of the sun, or a star, to determine the ship's position
Smack	A type of sailing fishing boat
Stanchion	Upright support made from wood or iron
Starboard	The right hand side
Stays'l	The inner of two heads'ls
Stern gland	Bearing carrying the propeller shaft through the hull
Storm trys'l	Small triangular sail for use instead of the mains'l in bad weather
Tackle	An arrangement of rope and blocks to give a mechanical advantage when pulling
Thwart	A bench or seat
Thwartships	Across the ship
Tiller	A spar attached to the rudder-head for steering
Toerail	Low wooden rail round the outside of the deck
Topping lift	Rope supporting the end of the boom
Tops'l	Small sail set above the mains'l
Topsides	The upper part (above the waterline) of a yacht's hull
Tripping line	Small line used to furl the roller jib
Truck	The top of the mast
Twin stays'ls	Used when running in place of the mains'l
Two blocks	When the blocks of a tackle come together
Wind vane	A wooden sail on top of the self steering gear to catch the wind
Windward	The windward side is the upwind side